JULIA McLEOD

PATCHWORK
LUXE

Quilts from Neckties, Kimonos & Sari Silks

C&T PUBLISHING
Another Maker Inspired!

Text and photography copyright © 2024 by Julia McLeod

Photography and artwork copyright © 2024 by C&T Publishing, Inc.

PUBLISHER: Amy Barrett-Daffin

CREATIVE DIRECTOR: Gailen Runge

SENIOR EDITOR: Roxane Cerda

ASSOCIATE EDITOR: Karly Wallace

TECHNICAL EDITOR: Del Walker

COVER/BOOK DESIGNER: April Mostek

PRODUCTION COORDINATOR: Zinnia Heinzmann

ILLUSTRATOR: Mary Flynn

PHOTOGRAPHY COORDINATOR: Rachel Ackley

FRONT COVER PHOTOGRAPHY by Craig Isaacs, BlueGoo Photography

SUBJECTS PHOTOGRAPHY by C&T Publishing, Inc

LIFESTYLE PHOTOGRAPHY by Craig Isaacs, BlueGoo Photography

INSTRUCTIONAL PHOTOGRAPHY by Julia McLeod, unless otherwise noted

Published by C&T Publishing, Inc., P.O. Box 1456, Lafayette, CA 94549

Library of Congress Cataloging-in-Publication Data

Names: McLeod, Julia Mary, 1965- author.

Title: Patchwork luxe : quilts from neckties, kimonos & sari silks / Julia McLeod.

Description: Lafayette, CA : C&T Publishing, [2024] | Summary: "In Patchwork Luxe, quilters will learn how to master the challenges of piecing patchwork with silk fabrics, how to source and care for silk textiles, and use different silk techniques. Readers will also find a handful of sample projects from bed-sized quilts to home decor items to quilt"-- Provided by publisher.

Identifiers: LCCN 2024008697 | ISBN 9781644034880 (trade paperback) | ISBN 9781644034897 (ebook)

Subjects: LCSH: Patchwork--Patterns. | Quilting--Patterns. | Patchwork quilts. | BISAC: CRAFTS & HOBBIES / Quilts & Quilting | CRAFTS & HOBBIES / Sewing

Classification: LCC TT835 .M47173 2024 | DDC 746.46/041--dc23/eng/20240402

LC record available at https://lccn.loc.gov/2024008697

Printed in China

10 9 8 7 6 5 4 3 2 1

Dedication

To our daughters, Hannah and Siân. You are the little geese who have flown yet still bring me joy every day. I love you.

Acknowledgments

Thanks are due to so many people; some who are as passionate as I am about quilting, and others who simply exercise patience each time I dive into yet another quilt project.

Quilters are my tribe: Thank you to the members of San Francisco Quilters Guild, East Bay Heritage Quilters and The San Francisco Sew and Sews. I find so much fun, friendship, and inspiration in these creative groups.

To all the stalwart program and workshop coordinators across the US and Canada who have hosted me virtually and in person—I've appreciated every opportunity to speak, teach, and travel.

To the quilt industry folks at Mancuso Show Management, Quilts, Inc., The Quilt Show, Creative Spark Online Learning and Hello Stitch Studios who have given me mile-stone opportunities: Your show of confidence has served to move me forward, creatively and professionally.

Writing this book has been one of those milestones. Thanks to Roxane Cerda and the whole team at C&T for their skill and support. I am grateful to my friends Laura and Lindy for allowing me to use their beautiful homes for a quilty photo shoot, and to my photographer, Craig Isaacs, for being such a pleasure to work with.

To my parents, Ian and Ruth McLeod, who were makers by necessity and by choice; thank you for providing me the privilege of pursuing a life in art and design.

Without a stable and happy home, I would not have had the chance to spend so many hours snipping up fabric and sewing it back together again. Thank you to Tony Phillips, my long-suffering 'quilt widower' for your love and forbearance.

CONTENTS

Half-Square Triangle Pillow

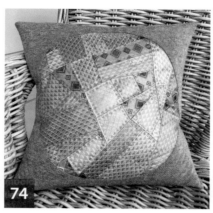

Crazy Circle Pillow

Mothers and Daughters
Bed Runner

Geese Crossing Mini Quilt

Every Which Way

Kaleidoscope Pineapple

Flying Circus

Stars Aligned

Rambling Rose Table Runner

Introduction

Welcome to *Patchwork Luxe!*

I'm a magpie, a sucker for shiny, luxurious things. To me, silk fabrics are like pebbles on the shore that have been left glossy by the waves. My eyes delight in the intense colors and luster of silk satins, brocades, jacquards, and more.

I quilted with cotton for many years, but after making my first all-silk quilt, I got hooked on working with these unique and lustrous textiles. There was no going back to the *dull side*!

When I visit quilt guilds to lecture or teach, I can guarantee that there will be quilters who have collected silk textiles while living overseas or traveling as tourists. Others have family members living abroad who have sent gifts of silk saris, sarongs, kimonos, or scarves. It's also common to find makers with bags of a late loved one's neckties that they can't bring themselves to part with.

All these special silks are kept reverently in drawers or boxes and brought out occasionally to be admired. But unless you have significant dressmaking experience, cutting and piecing with silk can be daunting. Silk fabrics stretch, slip, and fray in a way that our usual material of choice—quilters cotton—do not. All these factors serve to make the average quilter turn back and pack away the silk fabrics once again.

Let's bring those beautiful fabrics into the light. It is my hope that this book will give you the courage and know-how to reach for your scissors and turn those silk treasures into a beautiful, *luxe* piece of patchwork that you can use and enjoy. Happy Sewing!

SILK

What to Know About Silk

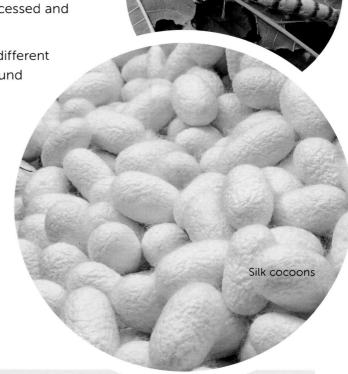

The Bombyx mori moth

Silkworms on mulberry leaves

Silk is an animal protein fiber secreted by moth larvae. This natural fiber is prized for its luster, strength, and absorbent qualities that make it easy to dye and print and for the ease with which it can be blended with other fibers.

Most commercially produced silk comes from the domesticated Bombyx mori moth that feeds on mulberry leaves. The cocoons created by these silkworms produce 109–328 yards (100–300m) of white silk filament, which is then processed and spun into silk thread.

Other species of silk worms, feeding on a variety of different plants, are the source of silk in smaller quantities around the world. Tussah, the best-known wild silk, is grown in China, Japan, North Korea, and South Korea. In Africa, you'll find Kalahari and sanyan silks; unique to Madagascar is landibé silk in shades of tan. Specific regions of India produce brown tussar silk, golden muga silk, and the heavier eri silk. The greenish Tensan silk is prized in Japan, while fagara silk grows in regions as far apart as China and Sudan.

Silk production, or *sericulture*, is an industry with high labor and production costs. China and India are currently the dominant producers, but such countries as Uzbekistan, Brazil, Japan, Republic of Korea, Thailand, Vietnam, and Iran also grow silk.[1]

Silk cocoons

PEACE SILK

Mahatma Gandhi extended his message of ahimsa, or nonviolence, to textiles: He promoted the wearing of cotton instead of silk, because most methods of silk production involve killing the larvae to harvest an unbroken filament from the cocoon. "Peace silk" is made on a small scale in India by processing the silk cocoons only after the moths have hatched and flown.

1. International Sericulture Commission

The History of Silk Fiber and Fabric

The earliest use of silk filament in textiles dates back to China's Neolithic period, around 3000 BCE. One legend has it that a Chinese princess accidentally dropped a silk cocoon into her hot tea and observed its unraveling, revealing the finest, longest filament she had ever seen.

Chinese silk production was fiercely protected for centuries before the secrets of sericulture were acquired by Japan, Korea, and India around 200 BCE.

Travelers on the *Silk Road*—trading routes that ran from China west through Persia and Eastern Europe to Italy—finally smuggled silkworm eggs and mulberry seeds to Turkey and Greece in the sixth century.

Sericulture was established in Spain by the tenth century and within 200 years had spread to northern Italy.

In the densely populated cities of Europe, by using imported raw materials from China and Persia, the silk spinning and weaving industry grew throughout the seventeenth and eighteenth centuries.

Meanwhile, in the Americas, Spain attempted to bring sericulture to Mexico and California in the early sixteenth century, and the 1700s saw attempts by England's King James I to establish silk production in the American colonies. From Connecticut to Georgia, mulberry trees were planted. Successful for a while, silk production ultimately gave way to a more profitable crop: tobacco.

The Silk Road

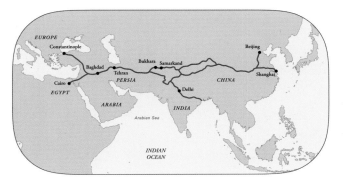

The Silk Road was a romanticized name for the well-worn trade routes that carried not only silk but horses, paper, spices, jade, glass, furs, and slaves between East and West.

Cocoons boiling

Although American sericulture faltered, the 1800s saw a strong U.S. textile industry employing imported silk to manufacture thread, ribbons, and textiles. Quilters incorporated silk scraps and ribbons into their crazy quilts, a style trend that remained popular for the last quarter of the nineteenth century.

This detail of a crazy quilt made by Myrtie Ballou in the late 1800s includes embroidered silk ribbon.

In the early twentieth century, Japan took the lead in using scientific methods to cultivate silk on farms and in factories. Those techniques are now used worldwide. Two world wars and the invention of *rayon*, or artificial silk, affected the production and sales of silk worldwide.

Throughout history, many and various factors have influenced the spread of sericulture and silk textile manufacture. Drought, flood, plague, war, trade embargoes, labor costs, and competing crops have all contributed to the success or failure of silk production.

THE HUGUENOTS

In the sixteenth and seventeenth centuries, religious persecution of the Huguenots, French reformed Protestants, led many skilled weavers to migrate to England, Germany, France, and the Netherlands. Walk around the Spitalfields neighborhood of London, and you can still see the attic weaving studios with their wide weavers' windows.

A Huguenot house in Spitalfields, London

Types of Silk Fabrics

To describe a fabric as silk doesn't tell us anything about its weight or texture. Typically, when people think of silk, they imagine a shiny satin. Satin is a weave structure that creates the most glossy surface and really exploits the lustrous sheen of the vertical warp threads. But not all satin is silk, and not all silk is satin. For example, when cotton is woven with a satin weave structure, it is usually called *sateen*. Although it does have a sheen, it's easy to distinguish from silk because it's a little more bulky and less lustrous.

Let's look in more detail at the variety of fabric types that are commonly made from silk.

Crepe de chine is a mossy weave with a matte finish. This fabric is most often used for dresses or blouses because it drapes beautifully. The subtle texture can be created by the twist of the yarn used or the way the threads are woven together.

Satin is a twill weave that brings more of the warp (vertical) threads to the surface. Satin can be fluid and drapey or heavy and quite stiff, depending on how tight the weave is.

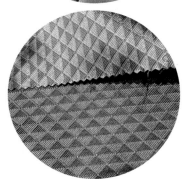

Jacquard is named for a type of loom. Jacquard fabrics feature a figured, woven design.

Damask is a type of jacquard weave that is fully reversible. The name of the fabric comes from Damascus, from where this textile was originally exported. Table linens are often made from damask cotton or linen.

Brocade is also woven on a jacquard loom and features designs that imitate embroidery and leave *floats* (looping threads) on the back.

Dupioni is a plain-weave, crisp, stable fabric that is characterized by its textured weft. The yarn is less processed, leaving lumpy slubs of silk to create interest.

Taffeta is similar in weight to dupioni silk, but without the natural texture; instead, taffeta is smooth and crisp.

Chiffon is a sheer, lightweight fabric often used for blouses or evening gowns.

Remember, any of these fabrics could equally be made using silk's most common imitators, rayon or polyester. It's common to find polyester versions of dupioni or crepe de chine, while rayon, the original "Artificial Silk," is often used to make satin or brocade.

◼ DIANA'S GOWN ◼

Princess Diana's 1981 wedding gown, made by David and Elizabeth Emanuel, was made from ivory English-woven taffeta. Alas, in the tight quarters of the glass coach in which Diana and her father traveled to St. Paul's Cathedral, the voluminous skirt and 25-foot train got thoroughly crushed. Both dress and train went down the aisle significantly wrinkled.

How to Distinguish Silk from Synthetics

It's very common to come across a shiny, drapey fabric and assume that it is silk.

Kind people frequently give me lengths of fabric from their travels in Japan, Indonesia, or India, telling me that it is silk when, in fact, the (often gorgeous) piece is polyester or rayon.

It's an honest mistake and doesn't render the fabric unusable for quilting, but polyester in particular does not piece into a quilt as easily as silk does. Polyester doesn't hold a crease and is also much more sensitive to a hot iron than is pure silk.

Rayon, first marketed as Artificial Silk, is less sensitive to heat than is polyester, although it will shrink if too much steam is used. Rayon fabrics are popular with dressmakers for their soft, drapey qualities, but quilters may just find rayon floppy and slippery! These qualities can be tamed by using the same techniques I recommend for working with silk.

▦ BEWARE MISLEADING LABELS! ▦

When harvesting fabric from garments, check the label to find out the fiber content. Mostly, the label is accurate, but not always. My favorite label, found on a necktie, says "100% Satin." This tells us nothing about the fiber content of the fabric, only the weave structure.

100% Satin!

If there is no label, the best way to determine whether your beautiful mystery textile is, in fact, made of silk is to light a candle and carry out a burn test.

Make sure you're in a well-ventilated room and always place the candle and conduct your burn tests over aluminum foil or a recycled pie pan to avoid accidental fires and surface damage. Be sure that your candle is unscented; one of the identifying features of a textile is the smell it gives off while burning.

Cut a small square of fabric and, using tweezers, hold it to the flame.

Hold the burning swatch over a pie pan or piece of foil and observe the following:

- How does the fabric ignite? Does it instantly flare up into a bright flame, or is it slow to catch fire?

- Does it self-extinguish when you move it away from the candle, or does it continue to burn?

- What color smoke is it giving off?

- How does it smell as it burns? (Caution: Don't inhale a lung-full of black smoke!)

- As it finishes burning, does the residue melt and drip, or does it leave ash? If the latter, what color is the ash?

- Is the remaining ash dusty or crunchy?

- Are you left with a hard, black plastic bead?

The Burn Test Chart below covers three main fiber groups: animal, plant, and man-made. A fourth category contains rayon, also known as viscose rayon, modal, acetate, lyocell, and bamboo. These fabrics are all made from cellulose extracted from wood pulp. Although that description makes it sound like a natural fiber, the process of turning wood pulp into thread is chemically intensive and often harmful to the environment. I consider rayon to be a hybrid fiber.

Use the Burn Test Chart to identify the various characteristics of your mystery fabric as it burns. The major flag to watch for is black, tarlike residue that hardens to a bead. That's a sure sign that your fabric is an oil product.

If you're really in love with a fabric that turns out to be polyester, the most common imitator of silk, it *is* possible to include it in your quilt project. However, you *must* remember to turn your iron down to a low heat setting to avoid accidental scorching, shrinking, or melting.

■ INKS, DYES, AND FINISHES ■

Remember, as you test pieces of fabric, they may contain chemical finishes, dyes, and inks. These factors can affect the way a swatch burns.

Burn Test Chart

Fabric	Flame	Smell	Residue
Cotton, Linen	Steady yellow/orange flame that continues to burn	Burning paper or leaves	Fluffy, gray ash
Wool	Orange, flickering flame with a tendency to self-extinguish	Burning hair	Brittle, dark gray ash
Silk	Slow, steady burn that might self-extinguish	Burning feathers	Crushed beads of ash that turn to powder
Rayon	Fast-burning flame that continues to smolder	Burning wood	Almost no ash
Polyester	Sputtering, orange flame that emits black smoke; fabric melts and drips rather than turning to ash	Chemical, sweet, or perfumed odor	Hard black beads that cannot be crushed

This information is an amalgam of many burn charts available on the internet.

Here is a simple summary:

- Plant fibers burn in a way that feels familiar to you if you've ever stood near a bonfire of wood, leaves, paper, or the like.

- Animal fibers, such as wool and silk, give off a smell of burning keratin that will remind you of that time you burned your bangs on a birthday cake candle or a curling iron.

- Man-made fibers burn in a way that you will want to move away from, emitting black smoke, a strong smell, and a melting residue.

Again, please exercise caution when burn-testing fabrics!

Burning polyester, melting and producing a black, tarlike residue

Sourcing Silk Fabrics

If you're already a quilter, it's likely you have built up a stash of quilters cotton purchased from your favorite local quilt store. As you venture into piecing silk quilts, you may feel hesitant to start a whole different stash of silk. The good news is that silk fabric can often be found cheaply in the form of thrift store finds, or even for free if you ask friends and neighbors for their unwanted silk clothing and neckties.

Put the word out via social media. I posted on social media and local online classified sites that I was in search of silk neckties. Within days, I had picked up dozens of ties from friends and neighbors who gladly thinned out their wardrobes—and it cost me nothing.

▌ BUILD CONNECTIONS ▐

I connected with a local thrift shop manager. She now regularly lets me know when to swing by and pick up bags of neckties. They're a slow-selling item here in California where every day is Casual Friday!

In your local thrift stores, seek out the evening-wear section for dupioni or taffeta skirts and the blouse racks for pretty crepe de chine prints. In larger thrift shops, you may be lucky enough to find an international clothing section of saris, tunics, and even kimonos.

Many towns have a recycling depot where art supplies and other items are available to creative types to upcycle.

Contact your local upholstery shop or interior designer. They may have scraps of silk decor fabrics.

Luxury dress fabric stores stock silk fabrics in various weights. Go shopping if you want to treat yourself to something special. I sometimes buy a yard of stunning fabric and back it up with fabric from my thrift store finds. See Stretching Your Stash (page 21) for ways to make any fabric go further.

Word of mouth is a powerful tool. I have become a magnet for silk just by telling friends, and you may too!

Be careful what you wish for!

Silk from neckties, kimonos, scarves, decorator fabrics, Chinese brocades, saris, and clothing

Harvesting Fabric from Garments and More

Some quilt artists whose work I admire, such as Sherri Lynn Wood and Zak Foster, use upcycled garments in their quilts and do nothing to disguise the fact that these textiles were once shirts, pants, and more. They exploit the arches and curves of armholes and necklines; they retain buttonhole plackets, cuffs, and pockets.

My way of working is to harvest fabrics from eclectic sources and use them as if they had come to me in the form of yardage. Textiles from neckties, saris, and kimonos can blend together in my quilts in a way that belies their origins.

The choice is yours regarding how to use your precious fabrics.

Whatever your approach, the techniques in this book will help you tackle the challenges of silk's tendency to stretch, slip, and fray, leaving you with results that are structurally stable and that accurately represent your vision.

Preparing your fabrics for cutting can differ, depending on the item. Tablecloths, curtains, sarongs, and saris need no deconstructing.

Kimonos are highly rewarding to pick apart. The kimono is a zero-waste garment. Take one apart, and you'll find that you have as many as 14 yards of fabric 14˝ or 17˝ wide, with only a small curve cut out at the neckline.

Silk blouses, jackets, pants, and dresses should be cut apart along the seams (unless there are seams you want to make a feature of) after they have been aired out, hand washed, or dry-cleaned. Neckties should be cleaned *after* they have been taken apart.

Neckties vary in their construction. The batting is rarely worth keeping, unless you have some kind of fiber art project in mind. The lining is usually lightweight polyester. Occasionally, it's silk and may be worth keeping.

Once you've opened up the tie, hold it up to the light to check for threadbare areas where the tie was folded, oily patches where the knot was tied under the chin, cigarette burns, and food stains. Most neckties I pick up in thrift stores have barely been worn and won't need cleaning. But if you're piecing a quilt from a beloved grandpa's tie collection, you may be working with some well-worn fabrics.

How to Deconstruct a Necktie

I use neckties a lot in my quiltmaking. Here's a quick and efficient way to take apart a tie. Don't waste time with a seam ripper—see how easy it is to pull out one simple thread and snip away the lining. Presto!

1. Find the two bar tacks, one at each end of the necktie. Cut them with a seam ripper. **A**

2. Remove the label and/or the tie loop. **B**

3. Locate the long, strong thread that runs through the seam. Cut it at each end. (In vintage ties, this may be a conventional seam that will require unpicking with a seam ripper.) **C**

4. Pull out the thread. **D**

5. Open the tie to expose the batting. **E**

6. Remove the batting. **F**

Most neckties take the form of a tube of bias-cut fabric with batting inside and a lining at each end.

A

B

C

D

E

F

7. Trim away the lining at each end. G

8. Unless you have other uses for the batting and lining (usually polyester), discard them. H I

Most neckties yield about as much fabric as a fat eighth of quilters cotton.

Stretching Your Stash

Once you have sourced fabrics from thrifted garments or textiles brought from faraway places, one thing is certain: When you run out, you can't buy more.

This finite quality of rescued materials can make planning a quilt challenging. You won't easily be able to follow a pattern that requires a 2-yard cut of one color and a fat quarter of four more.

Working with these kinds of materials requires us to improvise, to group like fabrics together that "read" similarly, and to stay flexible as we piece our patchwork. Obviously, a fabric stash of many neckties is well suited to any quilt design that could be described as scrappy. Neckties are long and narrow, so they lend themselves perfectly to striped and stripped blocks.

Kimonos and other garments yield more generously sized chunks of material. Consider using these fabrics in blocks and for areas like borders that require larger pieces of fabric.

A sari is usually about 5 yards long and often features a border on one or both of the long sides. The *pallu*, the decorative panel at one end, covers the head or hangs loosely over the shoulder.

In my quilts, I sometimes support the multitude of found fabrics with yardage of solid-colored dupioni silk. I buy it by the yard from online sources, including silkbaron.com,

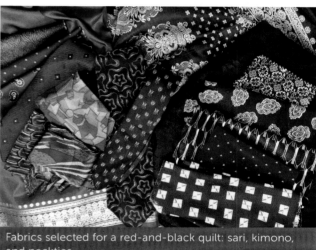

Fabrics selected for a red-and-black quilt: sari, kimono, and neckties

fabricwarehouse.com, or fabricwholesaledirect.com. It can be reassuring to know that you have enough plain fabric for sashing, creating a deep border, or binding.

It's often the case that a star fabric dictates the design of the quilt. If I want to fussy cut particular motifs from one gorgeous fabric, the number I can cut—three, four, eight?—might drive the composition of the quilt.

Although I use traditional blocks in my quilts, I think of myself as an improvisational quilter because I enjoy the challenge of making things up as I go along. It can be unnerving to begin a quilt without knowing how it will end up, but I encourage you to give it a try!

Combining Varied Textiles

When you're working with a variety of upcycled fabrics from garments, furnishings, saris, neckties, and more, a challenge may arise: Your chosen collection of fabrics may vary greatly in weight.

Imagine trying to combine a sturdy denim or a damask upholstery fabric with a blouse-weight crepe de chine or a silk sari; techniques are required to accommodate that imbalance.

The first (and fairly obvious) solution is to add an iron-on fusible interfacing to the lightest-weight fabrics. See Stabilize Your Fabrics with Fusible Interfacing (page 24) for my favorites.

Don't choose anything too hefty, but choose the right weight to "beef up" your lightest fabrics to match the weight of the heavier material. The resulting quilt top will be a little more bulky than one made from typical quilters cotton, so consider choosing a lightweight batting to compensate.

Another option is to gather all the lightest-weight fabrics together into detailed blocks with many seams (see Crazy Piecing into Panels, page 33). These blocks, with their many seam allowances, feel more substantial than a single section of lightweight silk. Create an overall design that alternates those pieced blocks with sections of heavier material.

The technique of fabric foundation piecing provides a substrate onto which a whole range of fabrics can be sewn. Pay attention to how you distribute your heaviest fabrics. If they're all clustered on one side of the block or on one side of the finished quilt, the contrast will be obvious. But if the heavy- and lightweight fabrics are evenly distributed, the finished quilt (with its batting, back, and quilting) will feel balanced.

Here's an example of a small quilt in which a crazy-pieced fabric I created from very lightweight silks and cottons was paired with denim in simple half-square triangles (HSTs).

Denim Diamond: The crazy piecing pairs lightweight crepe de chine and cotton shirting. This "made" fabric is then combined with denim in half-square triangles.

Batting, Backing, and Binding Choices

Batting is a personal choice. Every quilter has a different preference when it comes to loft (how puffy the quilt looks), weight, and drape.

The longarm quilters I work with often like to use wool batting in a silk quilt. It's lightweight and breathable, has a nice loft, and doesn't crease.

A lightweight cotton or 80/20 cotton/polyester blend is also a good choice.

I never use polyester batting because washability is not my prime concern.

I am drawn more to pattern than to texture, so I have even used preshrunk cotton flannel as batting. This choice results in a really skinny coverlet, similar to a nineteenth-century piano shawl. Bear in mind that my needs might be different from yours. As a traveling quilt instructor, one of my criteria is that a quilt folds up small into a suitcase.

I use quilters cotton for the backs of my quilts. Silk is expensive and slippery. You want that quilt to stay on the bed, not slip off! Save those silks for the top of the quilt.

My quilts usually have silk bindings, reinforced with fusible interfacing. Cut and attach as you would a cotton binding.

Cleaning and Caring for Silk

When my children were young and we had pets, I made cotton quilts and threw them in the washing machine. My home seemed to be full of dirty sports equipment and sharp claws! Everything changed when the kids left home and the old cat passed away. Our home became a quieter environment, and I had more time to sew. I turned to working with silk because I was willing to explore more complex techniques and because the resulting quilts wouldn't see harsh treatment.

Obviously, the safest use for a silk quilt is as a wallhanging, away from direct sunlight and greasy kitchen fumes.

Silk pillows should be seen as decorative rather than as cushions for the rumpus room, and a silk table runner should be removed before food is served. I have made several silk quilts that take the form of bed runners. Measuring about 40″ × 80″, they drape over the end of the bed beautifully and don't get tugged about like a full-size quilt might.

Silk textiles have a reputation for being fragile and hard to care for. However, the structure of silk fiber is a smooth filament that does not attract dirt. If dirt does accumulate, it comes out easily when the fabric is washed or dry-cleaned.

Putting silk in the washing machine generates too much agitation, as does wringing. Silk is weaker when wet and more prone to creasing, and its beautiful luster can be lost in a vigorous wash. I have only once washed a necktie in the washing machine. It came out like a dull-skinned snake! Never again!

Hand washing or a gentle soaking for 5 to 10 minutes in tepid water and mild detergent usually lifts out dirt successfully. Rinse well and lay the wet silk fabric on a towel, roll up the towel with the silk inside, and squeeze to remove excess moisture. Lay the silk out on a flat surface to air-dry. Do not dry silk in direct sunlight, as it may fade.

Dry-cleaning silk garments is often recommended by manufacturers because it lowers the risk that dyes will run or fade, and it retains the fabric's luster.

I have carried out sample tests on a piece of quilted silk. The results from dry cleaning were flawless; hand washing was pretty good, but left the sample a little crinkled. Machine washing left the fabrics looking crinkled and turned the lustrous surface matte. Unless this effect is one you like, take your silk textiles and quilts to the dry cleaner.

Julia's 4 S's of Quilting with Silk

There's no doubt that silk can be tricky to handle, especially if you're accustomed to sewing with quilters cottons. Silk fabrics have a tendency to fray; they slip and slide when under the needle of your sewing machine; and they stretch and shape-shift, even when you've tried your hardest to cut accurately. How can you tame these challenging qualities?

These are my four favorite tips and techniques that make silk fabrics easier to work with:

1. Increase the Seam allowance.

2. Stabilize fabrics with fusible interfacing.

3. Sew blocks onto a Substrate for support—a fabric foundation.

4. Experiment with Starch and other stiffeners.

Seam Allowance

If you're making a quilt with a fairly robust silk fabric that doesn't fray excessively (taffeta, for example), it's possible to piece it successfully by simply increasing your seam allowance from a typical quilters' quarter inch to a half inch. This gives you a wider "fray zone," and if you handle the quilt top with care before basting and quilting, your project will turn out beautifully.

Try using a pinking blade on your rotary cutter, or pinking shears, if you prefer. The zigzag edge cut by this kind of blade slows down fraying by creating a line of tiny bias cuts so the threads are less able to slip out of the weave.

A pinking blade and pinked seam

Stabilize Your Fabrics with Fusible Interfacing

WHAT'S WHAT

The words *iron-on* or *fusible* and *stabilizer* or *interfacing* are often used interchangeably. Pellon, the manufacturer of many iterations of this product, uses the term *fusible interfacing* for products that add more body to any fabric and stay in place. The word *stabilizer* may mean that the product is intended to be torn out or that it will dissolve when washed. Always check the product description before you buy.

Most quilters' go-to solution when making necktie quilts is to stabilize their silk fabrics by applying a fusible interfacing to the back. Interfacings are typically used by garment makers to stiffen collars and cuffs. They are sold with or without a coating of tiny dots of heat-activated glue. The heaviest interfacings are employed in the making of hats, pouches, and bags.

There's no doubt that adding a fusible interfacing reduces fraying and stretching. Once all your fabrics have this stabilizer fused to the back, you can cut and sew as if you were piecing with quilters cotton.

Take some time to buy the right kind of interfacing to add to silk fabrics. Always err on the side of lighter-weight products. Thicker fusible interfacings really change the feel of silk, making it crunchy or weirdly spongey, not to mention adding weight to the finished piece.

There is an array of available fusible interfacings. Most are made from nonwoven polyester, some are woven polyester, and some are woven cotton. The chart below reviews the various types I have experimented with and use most often.

Different Types of Fusible Interfacing

Name of Fusible Interfacing	Fabric Structure	Fiber Content	Width	Relative Price	My Comments
Pellon P44F	Nonwoven	Polyester	20″	$	Unbeatable for the price; lightweight and fuses well
Pellon 906F	Nonwoven	Polyester	20″	$$	Billed as "sheerweight" yet hard to distinguish from P44F
Pellon Shape Flex SF101	Woven	Cotton	20″	$$$	If you prefer natural fibers, this all-cotton option is a good choice.
Presto Woven Cotton	Woven	Cotton	22″	$$$	A slightly better quality than SF101
Presto Sheer	Woven	Cotton	36″	$$$	Gorgeously lightweight 100% cotton
Sewer's Dream	Knit	Polyester	30″	$$$	Similar to QS Fabric Prep
Quilter's Select Fabric Prep	Woven	Polyester	30″	$$$	Wonderful drape and super lightweight; ideal if you're piecing a wearable project

I support independent quilt shops. However, the big-box craft stores are the place to go to find a big selection of Pellon products—and to save money by using a coupon!

HOW TO APPLY FUSIBLE INTERFACING

Heat your iron to the setting recommended for wool or silk. Many fusible interfacings are made from nonwoven polyester that that will shrink or pucker if overheated.

A regular-size ironing board works fine, but if you have a larger ironing surface available, use it.

Fuse the glue side of the interfacing to the back of the silk fabric by following these steps:

1. Lay the interfacing *glue side up* on your ironing surface. You'll feel the tiny raised dots of glue on one side of the interfacing. **A**

2. Place the silk fabric *right side up* on top of the interfacing. **B**

3. Lay a silicone pressing sheet on top, creating a third layer. Take care not to nudge the silk fabric out of position. The silicone pressing sheet will protect your iron from getting sticky with glue or from transferring small amounts of glue to the right side of the silk. **C**

4. Using a dry iron set on medium heat, press the silk to the interfacing with a slow "stomping" motion, holding the iron in place for three or four seconds before lifting and repositioning the silicone layer and the iron. Do not smooth the iron back and forth, as doing so might move the piece of fabric. **D**

5. Lay out several pieces edge to edge over the surface of the interfacing, jigsaw-style, as much as the size of your pressing surface allows. **E**

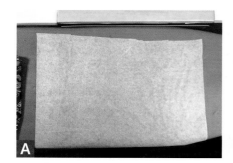

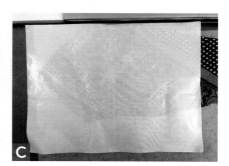

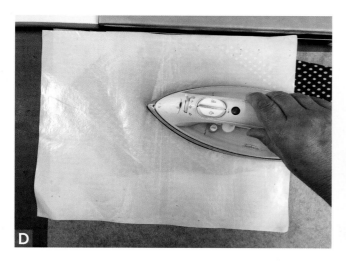

6. Once the silk is fused to the interfacing, remove the pressing sheet, trim away any excess interfacing from around the silk pieces, and press them one more time to make sure that all the interfacing has adhered. **F**

7. Use leftover scraps of interfacing to fill in any unfused sections. **G**

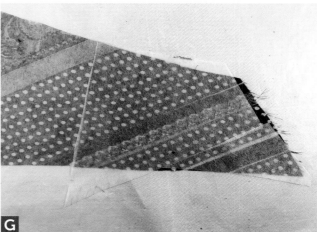

OOOPS!

Did you melt some polyester onto your iron? Did you press the glue side of the interfacing by mistake? Is your iron covered in a sticky mess?

Help is at hand: A regular dryer sheet—the sort you throw in the dryer with your laundry to soften and scent it—is all you need.

Turn up the heat on your iron to cotton or linen and smooth it back and forth on the dryer sheet. The oils and chemicals in the dryer sheet will remove all the gunk from the sole plate of your iron. ▶ Magic!

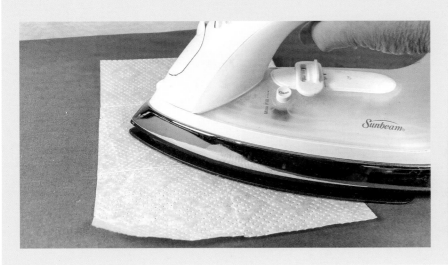

If you have a large piece or yardage of silk fabric, it may be easier to apply fusible interfacing as follows:

1. Lay out the fabric on your pressing surface, *wrong side up*, and place the fusible on top, *glue side down.* **A**

2. Press with a "stomping" motion, pressing one area before moving on to the next. **B**

3. Turn the fabric over and iron on the right side to make sure that the interfacing has completely fused to the fabric. **C**

I know many quilters who add fusible interfacing to several yards of silk fabrics at a time.

With the addition of fusible interfacing, it's possible to cut and sew as if using quilters cotton. The slip, stretch, and fraying qualities of silk are all mitigated when interfacing is added.

Use of a Substrate for Support

The traditional American art of fabric foundation piecing is less well known than the technique of foundation paper piecing. Paper piecing is not suited to silk patchwork because the ripping out of paper foundations stresses seams and leaves them exposed to fraying. Fabric foundations stay in place, giving accuracy in piecing, stabilizing the finished piece, and leaving most raw edges locked safely away between the face of the block and the fabric foundation on the back.

There are several ways to piece a block onto a fabric foundation, and I cover them all in Traditional Fabric Foundation Piecing (page 37).

- Draft your own foundation onto lightweight muslin.

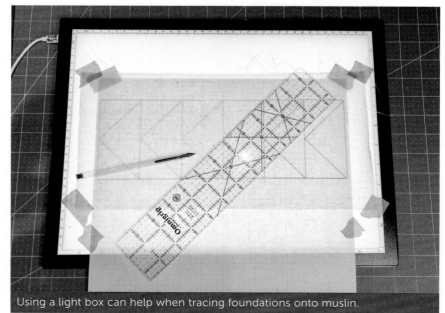

Using a light box can help when tracing foundations onto muslin.

- Use a commercially printed fabric foundation.

- Make string blocks by piecing onto a foundation of striped fabric, using the woven or printed design as your guide.

- Stitch onto a fabric foundation "freestyle," with no markings at all.

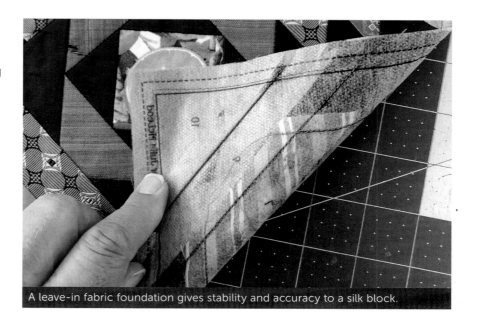

A leave-in fabric foundation gives stability and accuracy to a silk block.

Starch and Other Stiffeners

Silk's drapable quality that is so pleasing in a silk shirt or dress translates to a floppy nightmare for a quilter!

Treating silk fabric with a stiffening agent, usually referred to as *starch* or *sizing*, can make slippery fabrics much easier to cut and sew. Several spray-on products are available on the market. I don't recommend traditional starch, as it seems to leave flecks of a shiny residue, and if it's not washed out thoroughly, it can attract bugs.

Starch alternatives include Mary Ellen's Best Press and Acorn's Easy Press Fabric Treatment. The latter can turn a sloppy crepe de chine into something as crisp as taffeta. A product called Terial Magic gives paper-stiff results that might be perfect for appliqué projects or for crafting three-dimensional flowers or lampshades, but I think it's overkill for our purposes.

All these treatments should be washed or dry-cleaned out of the finished quilt. It's worth remembering that if you plan to treat your silks with any of these spray products, they will darken the color of the fabric. Make your color choices before spraying.

Two starch alternative sprays I sometimes use: Acorn's Easy Press Fabric Treatment and Mary Ellen's Best Press. A diffuser spray bottle gives a nice, fine mist.

TECHNIQUES

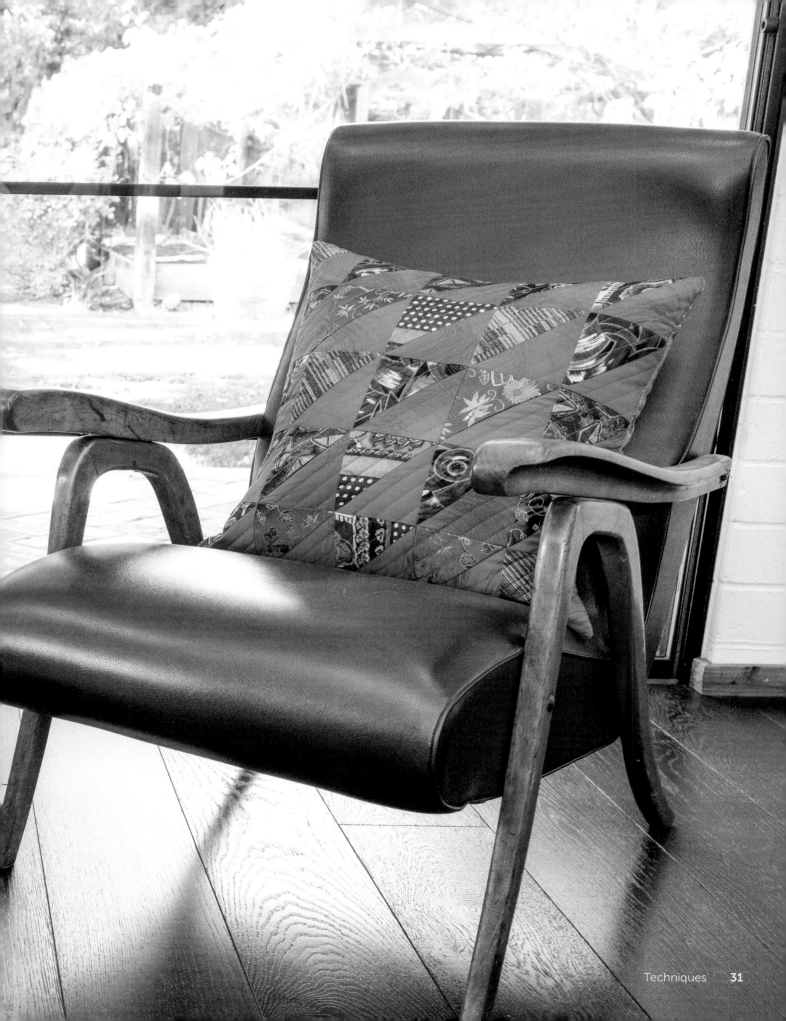

Traditional Machine Piecing with Fused Silks

Once you have applied fusible interfacing to silk fabrics, it's possible to cut, sew, and press as you would if you were working with quilters cotton. The good news is that you can use any traditional quilt pattern without adjusting for larger seam allowances. Be sure to have your iron on the silk setting to avoid scorching the polyester fusible interfacing. A little steam is helpful when pressing seams.

Follow these step-by-step instructions to make HSTs. The HST is beautifully simple and versatile. The Half-Square Triangle Pillow (page 70) is an easy project that uses this block.

1. To make 2 HSTs, begin with 2 squares ⅞″ larger than the desired finished block size. I am making 4″ finished squares (4½″ unfinished), so I have cut my squares 4⅞″. Draw a line diagonally across the wrong side of 1 square. **A**

2. Pin 2 contrasting squares right sides together. **B**

3. Sew 2 seams ¼″ on either side of the diagonal line. **C**

4. Cut along the diagonal line. **D**

5. Press the seam allowance toward the lighter-weight *or* the darker of the two fabrics. **E**

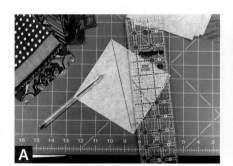

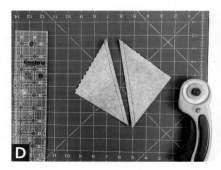

Crazy Piecing into Panels

This improvisational technique I developed works best if you don't sweat every decision: Pair fabrics, cut them, pair them again, and so on. You can choose to leave the patches quite large or keep on slicing and reattaching to create the effect of a mosaic of small pieces.

When selecting your fabrics, consider color choices. A low-contrast, analogous color palette comes together quite easily because everything coordinates. If you choose fabrics with strong contrasting colors and patterns, you will have to keep an eye on how they appear in the crazy piecing. Avoid having the same fabric meet up with itself; try to disperse everything evenly.

An analogous color palette with larger patches

High-contrast, scrappy fabric choices with smaller patches

1. Begin by selecting 8 pieces of fabric. In this case, I'm using neckties. If you're using fabric from a garment or yardage, cut chunks about 7″ × 12″.

2. Apply fusible interfacing to any lightweight silks that seem flimsy and stretchy. Sturdy woven brocades, jacquards, and damasks do not need fusible interfacing. **B** **C**

3. Match your 8 fabrics into 4 pairs (remember, don't sweat this decision! You'll be slicing them apart again before long!). Create 1 straight edge on each piece of fabric. **D**

4. Pin pairs with right sides together, matching the straight edges. Not all the fabrics will be the same dimension, but that's not important. Do not trim them down. **E**

5. Sew a ½″ seam along the straight edge of each pair. Note that for this technique, I recommend using a larger seam allowance because at times you will be joining fused fabrics with more robust fabrics that haven't been stabilized. The larger seam allowance lets your seams lay flatter once pressed. **F**

6. Press the seams open. Doing so distributes bulk as we continue to piece. Do not neaten up the odd-shaped edges. **G**

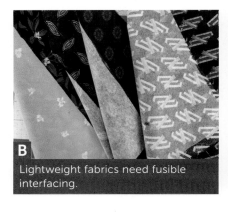
Lightweight fabrics need fusible interfacing.

Sturdier woven silks do not need fusible interfacing.

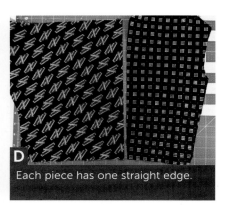
Each piece has one straight edge.

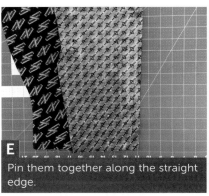
Pin them together along the straight edge.

Sew a ½″ seam along the straight edge.

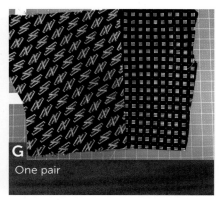
One pair

7. Now, you have 4 pairs. Cut each pair in half, cutting a little catawampus and avoiding 90-degree angles. **H** **I**

8. Switch the pairs around to create 4 four-patches. Join the straight edges together with a ½˝ seam, pressed open. Here, you can pay no attention to seams matching up, or you can take the trouble to match them if you want. A mix of both choices makes for an interesting crazy-pieced effect. **J**

9. Reach for your rotary cutter again and slice the four-patches any way you see fit. The goal is only to create a new straight edge to match with another straight edge. Avoid cutting through areas where 2 seams meet up because doing so will create bulk in your next seam. **K**

10. Join the four-patches together, matching the straight edges. Now we've created what I call *panels*. These panels are often shaped very strangely. Continue to create 1 straight edge to join with another. Keep the scraps as you trim. **L** **M** **N** **O**

H — Four pairs

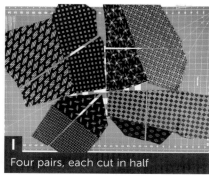
I — Four pairs, each cut in half

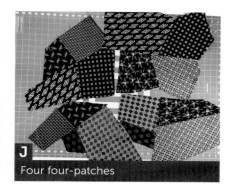
J — Four four-patches

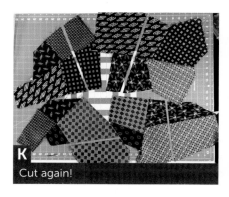
K — Cut again!

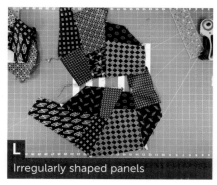
L — Irregularly shaped panels

M — Panels, each with one straight edge

N — Panels sewn together

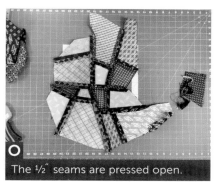
O — The ½˝ seams are pressed open.

11. Continue to neaten up 1 straight edge at a time. **P**

12. Join the panels together and watch your piece of crazy piecing grow. **Q**

13. Use the trimmings and scraps to add around the sides where corners are missing or edges are irregular. **R**

14. From your crazy-pieced panel, cut the shapes you need for your project. **S**

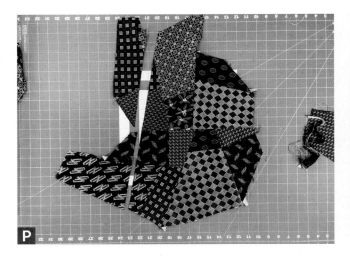

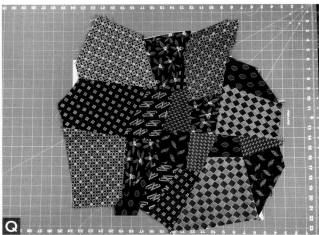

Rescue the scraps to sew onto corners or fill gaps.

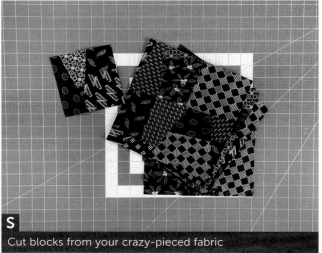
Cut blocks from your crazy-pieced fabric

Traditional Fabric Foundation Piecing

Foundation piecing onto paper is a popular method of piecing blocks. It produces accurate and sometimes intricate blocks that can be used in every style of quilt—traditional, modern, or art.

I have never loved the chore of ripping out the paper from the back of the block. When you're working with silk, the blocks don't like it either. Seams are stressed, and edges fray.

When the foundation is made of fabric, it can be left in as a supportive substrate that keeps the block stable, strengthens seams, and locks away fraying edges.

If the foundation is cut on the straight grain of the fabric (parallel with the selvedge), the silk pieces can be cut with the grain going in any direction. They can be super-stretchy and slippery, but once they're stitched down onto the leave-in foundation, the resulting block is as stable as if it were made of quilters cotton.

Try this technique. I promise you'll get beautiful results!

FOUNDATION BLOCK DESIGNS

Any block that can be made by using the paper-piecing technique can be made by using a fabric foundation. If you have books and patterns for paper piecing, trace them onto fabric (using a lightbox, if that helps) to make a fabric foundation. Complex patterns have numbers, showing in which order to sew things down.

You can approach fabric foundation piecing in several ways. This chapter shows you how to draft from scratch. You can also trace a strip of 4 Flying Geese blocks, using the Large Flying Geese Strips Foundation template (page 122). Use a light box if that helps you see through the fabric as you trace. I also show two preprinted products currently available; we explore making foundations out of striped fabric; and we try free-styling, following no lines at all.

Let's start from scratch and make our own foundations. The basic Flying Geese block is a super-easy design to start with because there are just three repeating seams.

I call each large triangle the "goose." For every goose, there are two smaller triangles, which I call the "background triangles."

Here, I'm demonstrating with a strip of four 2″ x 4″ blocks. You can make your geese units any size you like and make the string of geese as long as you want. This strip of four appears in the small *Geese Crossing Mini Quilt* (page 82) and in the *Every Which Way* quilt (page 86).

Note: For this technique, none of the silk needs to have fusible interfacing applied. The fabric foundation gives sufficient strength and stability to the block.

I use my rotary cutter freehand, following the lines on my cutting mat. Even if I were to use my ruler and cut as accurately as possible, silk has a way of shape-shifting. Squares become diamonds as soon as you pick them up! This technique gets its accuracy from the lines drawn on the foundation. The cutting dimensions given allow for a generous ¼″ seam as you sew and flip to create the strip of geese. The *outer* seam allowance of the block is ½″.

Your work will look its best if you press each seam after sewing.

Set up your workspace in a convenient way that allows you to cut, sew, and press each short seam without having to cross the room to do so (unless you want to add steps into your day!).

1. Cut a piece of lightweight, preshrunk muslin 5½″ × 9½″. This block will be trimmed to 5″ × 9″ unfinished, 4″ × 8″ finished with a ½″ outer seam allowance. Tape the muslin to your cutting mat. With a ballpoint pen, using the lines on the cutting mat as a guide, draw a rectangle 4″ wide and 8″ tall. **A**

2. Divide the rectangle into a stack of 4 boxes, each 4″ wide and 2″ tall. **B**

3. Draw a faint line down the center of the block, creating 8 boxes 2″ × 2″. Beware: This center line is a guide, not a sewing line. Draw it faintly or even in another color pen so that you don't make the mistake of sewing along it later. **C**

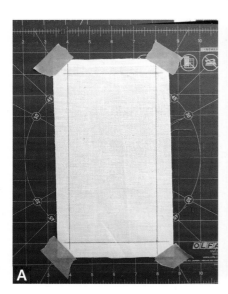
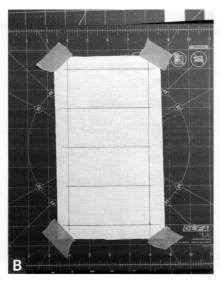
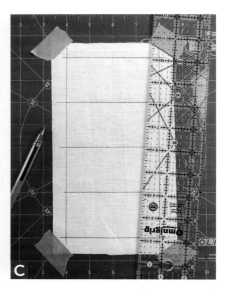

4. From the top center of each 2″ box, draw a diagonal line out to the lower, outer corners. Doing so creates a stack of 4 Flying Geese blocks. **D**

5. You will need 4 large triangles to make the "geese." Cut 2 squares 4½″ × 4½″ and then cut them again diagonally. Use the same fabric or make it scrappy by mixing prints. **E** **F** **G**

6. Choose a contrasting color for the background (some quilters refer to these sections as the wings of the geese). For a strip of 4 geese, cut 4 squares 3½″ × 3½″. Cut them diagonally to make 8 triangles. **H** **I**

7. From a piece of lightweight cardstock, create a line guide by drawing one dark, horizontal line approximately across the center. The placement of the line isn't important, but it does need to be a straight, dark line.

This line guide will allow you to see the drawn lines through the muslin foundation so you can position each piece accurately.

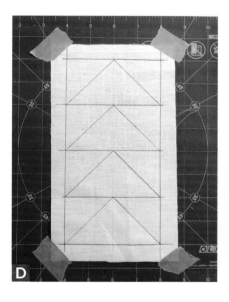

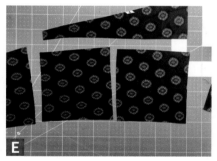

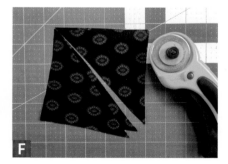

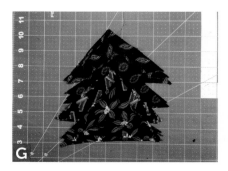

Place the foundation *inked side down*. We will be pinning the fabric on the unmarked side and flipping the block over to sew along the drawn lines.

8. Begin by pinning the first goose in place. Make sure that it is pointing *up*, not down. Using the white surface of the line guide, check that the silk triangle covers all the seam lines on the foundation.

9. The first seam is one of the 2 short sides of the goose. Slide the foundation into place on the line guide so that the seam line on the foundation aligns with the line drawn on the line guide. Peel back 1 side of the goose to see it clearly. The line guide will show an extended line either side of the block, indicating where the sewing line is.

10. I have sewn thousands of these Flying Geese, but I still position the background triangle where it's going to go. This step gives me the opportunity to make sure that the grain is running in the direction I want it to (in this case, vertically).

You may have chosen a fabric with no nap or noticeable grain, in which case you won't have this concern. This moment is also a chance to make sure that you're about to sew the *long* side of a background triangle to a *short* side of a goose.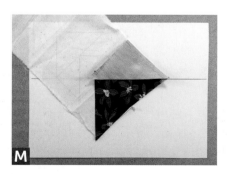

11. Flip the background triangle, using the sewing line as an axis, so that right sides are together. Remember, we are not matching raw edges, as in conventional piecing. Observe the line guide that shows you where your seam line will run. Allow a generous ¼″ seam. Pin in place.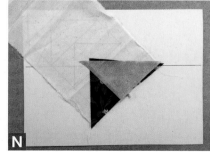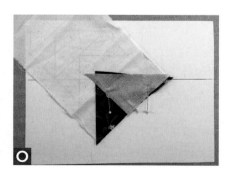

12. Flip the block over. The red dotted line here shows where to sew. Sew along the drawn line, starting ¼˝ before and ending ¼˝ after the seam line. **P** **Q** **R**

13. Flip the block to the right side and press. **S**

14. Check for shadowing if darker shades are going to show through a lighter fabric. Trim away excess, if necessary. **T** **U**

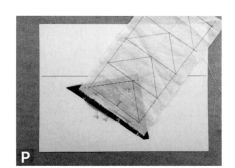

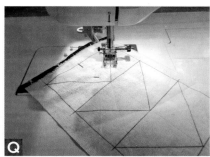

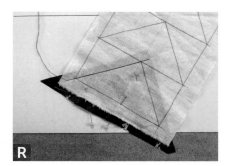

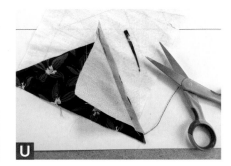

15. Line up the second seam with the line guide. **V**

16. Position the second background triangle and pin in place. **W**

17. Flip the block over, sewing along the printed line as before, starting and ending about ¼˝ from the start and finish of the seam line. **X**

18. Press the second background triangle in place. You will notice that the edges of the silk pieces are pretty irregular. None of that matters, as long as each piece overlaps the sewing lines successfully. **Y**

19. Ready for the next goose: Lay it down and eyeball how it's going to look. **Z**

20. Line up the horizontal sewing line with the line guide. **AA**

21. Place the goose pointing down and with the fabric right side down, lining it up so that the seam line runs through it with a generous ¼˝ allowance. Remember, with this technique, we are not matching edges. Pin in place. **BB**

22. Flip the block and sew along the horizontal seam line. **CC**

23. Assuming that the silks you are using are lightweight, there is no need to trim seams. You may want to trim away the little "ears" that show here at the top of the triangle to reduce bulk. **DD**

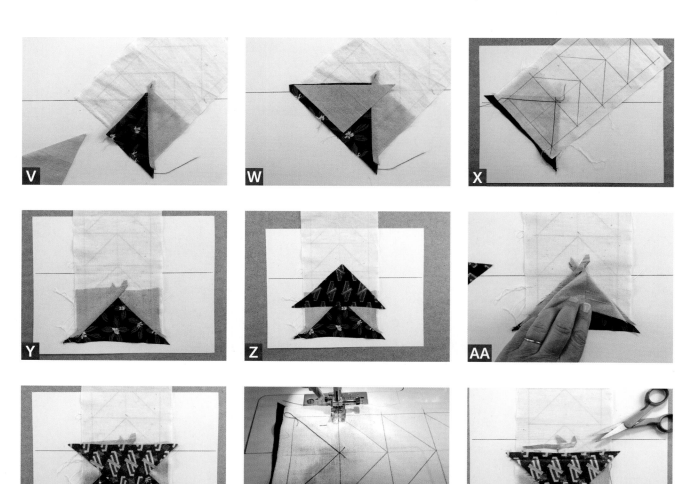

24. Press the goose up. 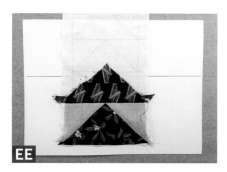 EE

25. Return to Step 10 and continue building this block, triangle by triangle. In this next round, we have the previous goose to help line up the background triangles. Notice how the tip of the background triangle aligns with the diagonal seam in the first block? This reference point is helpful for making sure that the background triangle is correctly positioned. FF

Congratulations! You have completed 1 strip of 4 Flying Geese. Know that as you repeat this technique, you will speed up. It's also possible, when making multiple blocks, to set them all up and execute the same step, sewing the same seam on repeat instead of just once.

FOUNDATION FABRICS

I used lightweight muslin in this example. You can use any light-colored cotton fabric in your stash. It's also possible to trace onto starched cotton lawn or nonfusible interfacing if you prefer a really sheer foundation.

Experiment with photocopying foundations onto fabric. I find that prepared paper-backed fabric is a little too dense and hard to sew through. I have fused fabric onto freezer paper and sent it through the printer with mixed results!

Two Commercially Printed Fabric Foundations

For those of you who have no wish to spend time drafting your own fabric foundation blocks, help is at hand! Preprinted products allow you to cut out the blocks and get sewing. Here are two of my favorites.

The first, like the DIY method shown in Traditional Fabric Foundation Piecing (page 37), is printed onto cotton muslin. The product, *Foundation by the Yard*, was designed by Sharon Hultgren and produced by Benartex. It's sold by the panel—usually about 1¼ yards long—and, depending on the design, one panel often yields sufficient blocks to make a crib-size quilt.

Be sure to prewash the panel and true up the blocks to 90-degree angles with a steam iron before sewing onto it. This product is ideal if you are working with lightweight silks. If your block contains quilters cottons, flannel, or any other substantial fabric, bear in mind that the finished project may be a little heavy; your quilt top has two layers of fabric, after all. Mitigate this extra weight by choosing lightweight batting.

Foundation by the Yard is rarely stocked by brick-and-mortar quilt shops. Search online to find a supplier near you. I regularly purchase this product from **rossvillequilts.com**

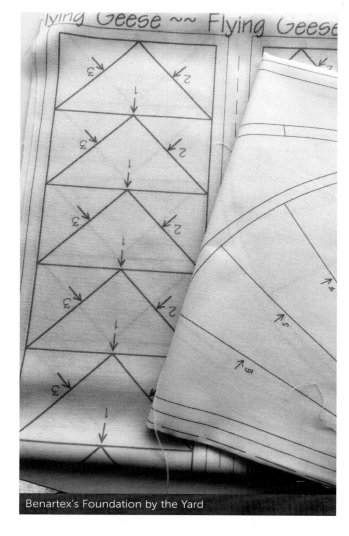
Benartex's Foundation by the Yard

A featherweight foundation that I love to use is a printed nonwoven polyester product by EZ Piecing. Accurate and lightweight, this foundation is ideal for wearable projects because it really is as light as a feather. Turn your iron down to the wool or silk setting to avoid scorching the polyester. You can purchase this product at **ezpiecing.com**

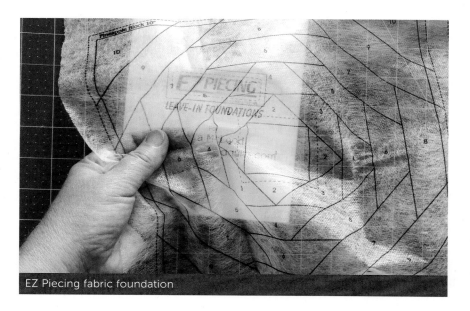
EZ Piecing fabric foundation

Piecing the Pineapple Block

Follow the steps on the next page to make a classic Pineapple block. You can trace the Kaleidoscope Pineapple Pineapple Block template (page 120) onto lightweight muslin, or you can purchase and use the Pineapple Kaleidoscope block design foundation I developed for EZ Piecing. This block is highly versatile and can look dramatically different, depending on color and value placement.

If this is your first Pineapple block, I recommend that you choose two colors, with one for the strips that run diagonally. In this example, these are orange (color A). The second color is for the strips that run parallel to the sides of the block. In this example, these are blue (color B). For the sample block I used a scrappy selection of orange necktie silks and a solid blue kimono fabric. Choose a third color for the center square (color C). In traditional Pineapple and Log Cabin blocks, this is usually red. Here, I fussy cut the center square from a citrus print.

For one block, cut as follows from 2″ strips, unless indicated otherwise.

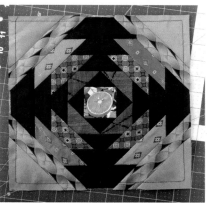

Pineapple Block Cutting Instructions

Piece #/ Round	How many to cut	Size to cut	Notes
1	1	2¾″ × 2¾″	Center Square, Color C
2	4	2″ × 2½″	Color B
3	4	2″ × 3¾″	Color A
4	4	2″ × 3¾″	Color B
5	4	2″ × 4¾″	Color A
6	4	2″ × 4¾″	Color B
7	4	2″ × 5¾″	Color A
8	4	2″ × 5¾″	Color B
9	4	2″ × 7″	Color A
10	1	6″ × 6″	Cut diagonally twice to make 4 corner pieces. Color A

1. With the foundation right side up, so you can read the numbers, position the center square (color C) right side up, so that it covers all 4 sides of the center square on the foundation. Hold it in place with a dab from a glue stick. Use a line guide (simply a piece of white paper or cardstock with one dark line drawn on it) or the lines on your cutting mat to determine where the sewing lines are. **A** **B**

2. **Round 2:** Position 1 strip of color B with right sides together along 1 side of the center square. Use the line guide or the lines on your cutting mat to see where the seam line will run. Allow a scant ½″ seam. Pin in place. **C**

3. Flip the entire block over and sew from the back along the seam line between pieces 1 and 2 where the fabric is pinned. Start ¼″ before and end ¼″ after the seam line begins and ends. **D**

4. On an ironing surface, press open the seam just sewn. **E**

5. In the same way, position, pin, and sew strips to the other 3 sides of the center square. **F**

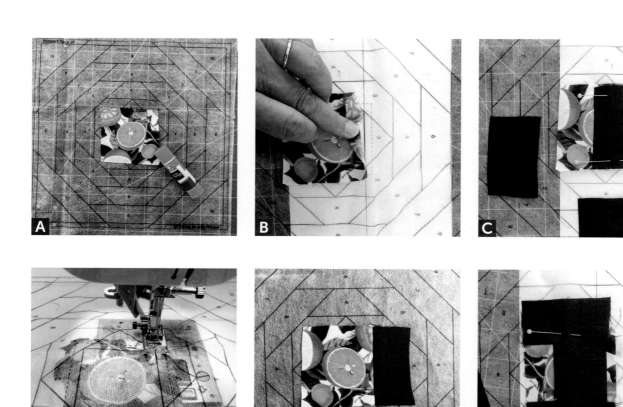

6. **Round 3:** Now, we are attaching diagonal strips. Use the line guide to find the next seam line. **G**

7. Pin 1 strip (color A) in place. **H**

8. Flip the whole block over and sew from the foundation side as before, along the seam line where the strip of fabric is pinned. *Do not press open yet.* **I**

9. Attach a second strip opposite the one just sewn. **J**

10. Now, some trimming is required. With the block face down, peel back the foundation along the seams you just stitched. Carefully trim away excess seam allowance. This process doesn't need to look pretty—I usually cut freehand. If you are using lightweight silks, very little bulk will build up. Double-check to make sure that a dark fabric isn't shadowing through a light one. **K**

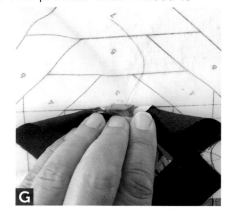

11. Flip the block over and press open the 2 diagonal strips. **L**

12. Pin, sew, trim, and press open the remaining 2 sides of this round. **M**

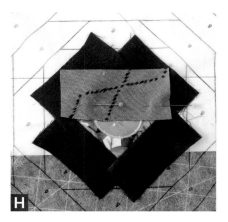

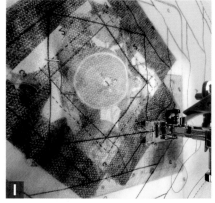

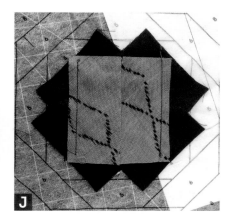

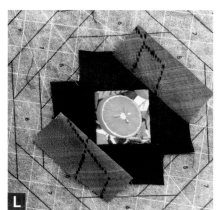

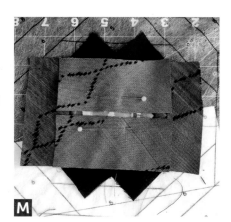

13. Continue to add, round-by-round, strips of color A and color B. By Round 6, you will have enough room to pin all 4 sides in place. I still recommend sewing each seam separately; don't try to stitch around in one big square because you're likely to catch down other strips. **N**

14. Round 10 is the final round, adding the corner triangles. Pin, flip the block over, and sew in place. Press open. **O** **P**

15. Staystitch around the edge of the finished block, ⅛" outside the seam line. Trim to leave a ½" seam allowance. **Q** **R** **S**

My *Kaleidoscope Pineapple* quilt (page 90) is still a grid of just nine Pineapple blocks. The careful color choices and fussy cutting are what make it special.

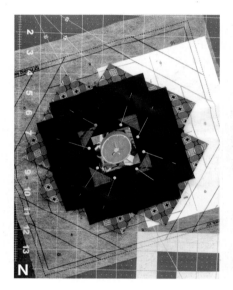

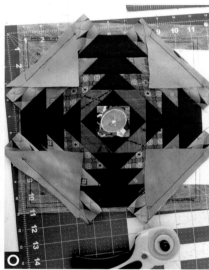

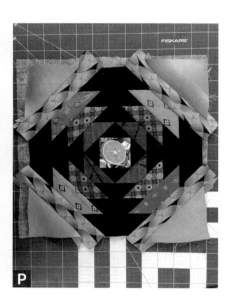

Notice that the EZ Piecing foundation shows a ¼" seam allowance. That's fine if you're piecing with cotton, but I always recommend a ½" seam allowance for silk blocks.

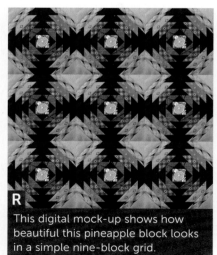

This digital mock-up shows how beautiful this pineapple block looks in a simple nine-block grid.

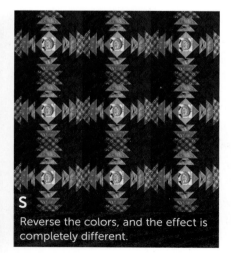

Reverse the colors, and the effect is completely different.

Piecing Grandmother's Fan

The Grandmother's Fan block appears in three of the projects in this book. It's a traditional block that is well suited to using scraps and for fussy cutting. The quarter fan is a versatile shape. I often bring four together to make a circle, sometimes with the addition of strips of Flying Geese or sashing. Don't be intimidated by the curves. Use plenty of pins or dots of fabric glue. I know a quilter who exclusively uses Acorn's SeamAlign Gentle Hold Fabric Glue. She likes it because there are no bumpy pins to distort the seams or damage her sewing-machine needle. I invite you to try both methods and conquer the curve!

In these steps, I'm once again using a product by EZ Piecing. Benartex also has a panel of Foundation by the Yard for this block, or you can trace your own from the Grandmother's Fan Foundation template (pages 120–121).

1. To aid in cutting the fan blades, cut a template from paper or clear lightweight plastic to cut around with a generous ¼″ seam allowance. **A**

2. I have chosen to alternate 2 fabric choices: a red silk repeating stripe and a polyester floral print. **A**

3. Place the fabric right side up and position the template as desired. Mark the template to make cutting subsequent pieces easier. **C D**

4. Each fan needs 6 blades. **E**

5. Position the fabric foundation on the line guide. **F**

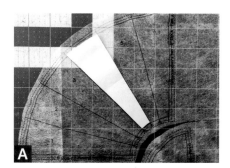

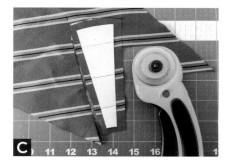

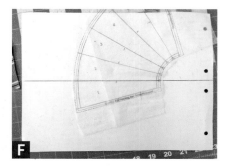

6. Pin the first fan blade in place.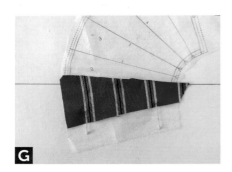

7. Place the second fan blade right side down on top of the first. Pin in place. Raw edges do not need to align. Pay attention to where the sewing line is, indicated by the line guide. **H**

8. Flip the entire block over and sew the first seam, starting and ending about ¼" from the start and finish of the seam line. **I**

9. Press the fan blade open. If you're using the EZ Piecing foundation, be sure to keep your iron set on a reduced heat so you don't scorch or shrink the polyester foundation. **J**

10. Trim away any darker fabric that might shadow through to the front. **K**

11. Using the line guide, position the block to add the third fan blade. **L**

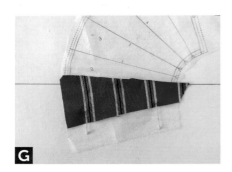
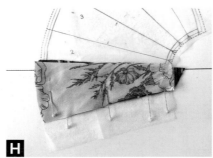
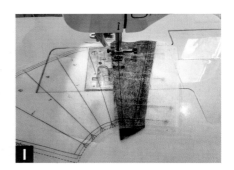

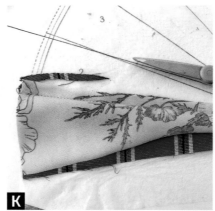
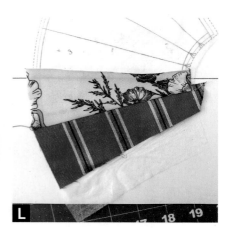

12. Pin the third fan blade in place and continue to pin, flip, sew, and press until all 6 fans are in place. Trim both curved edges. Leave the straight sides untrimmed. **M** **N**

13. Pin the shoulder pieces (Part B) onto the wrong side of your chosen fabric. Baste along the curve, ⅛″ from the seam line, in the seam allowance. Trim only the curved edge. **O** **P**

14. Place the fan right side up, lining up the straight seam on the line guide. Place the shoulder piece right side down on top, lining up the short seam line with the line guide and the trimmed edge with the outer edge of the fan. **Q** **R**

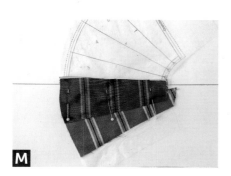

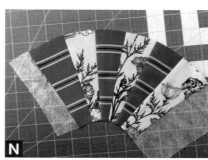

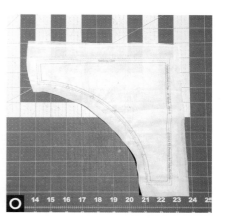

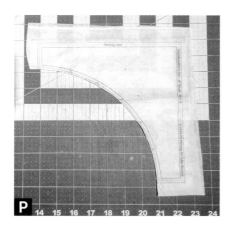

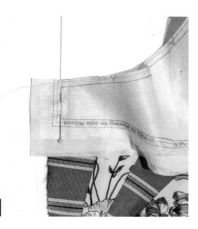

15. Do the same on the opposite side of the fan and then pin the 2 curved edges together, matching notches on the shoulder with seam lines on the fan. Add as many pins as you like to connect the 2 curves. **S** **T**

16. Sew the seam, removing pins as you go and avoiding any pleating with the use of a stiletto or scissors. **U**

17. Clip the curved seam every ½˝ or so. **V**

18. Press the seam toward the shoulder, leaving the fan flat. **W** **X**

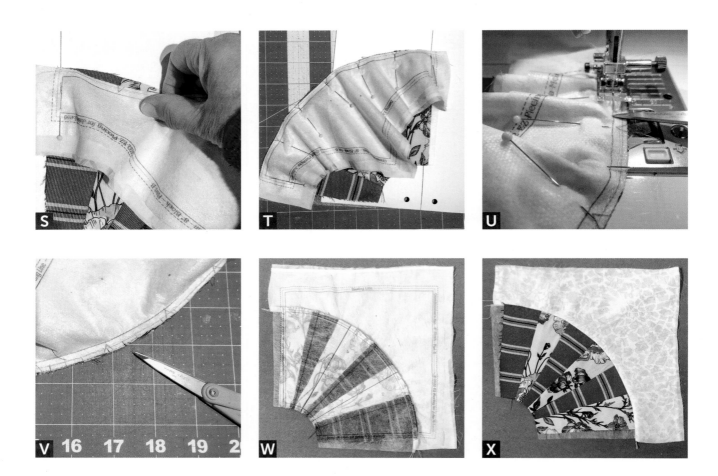

19. Place the center quarter-circle of the fabric foundation onto the wrong side of your chosen fabric. Baste and trim the curved edge. **Y**

20. Pin the center of the quarter-circle to the center seam of the fan's inner curve. **Z**

21. Align the side seams and pin in place. Add more pins along the curve. **AA** **BB**

22. Sew along the curved seam, removing pins, then clip, and press the seam toward the corner. Trim the block. **CC** **DD**

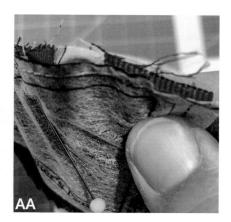

Alternative Fabric Foundation Applications

Using Striped Fabrics as Foundations

Printed and color-woven striped fabrics are fabric foundations just waiting to happen! See what stripes you have in your stash. Even the ugly ones can make great foundations because the colors will be on the back and won't show.

Here's what I did with a striped fabric I found in my stash and some scraps of dupioni silk a friend handed off to me when she was done making pillows.

This uneven stripe will give an asymmetrical result.

Dupioni silk is nice to work with because there is no right or wrong side.

1. From a printed striped fabric, cut strips on a 45-degree angle, as wide as the squares you wish to piece. These were 6½" wide. **A**

2. Cut the strips of striped fabric into squares. The printed stripe should run diagonally across each square. **B**

3. With the striped foundation printed side down, position the first scrap of fabric. You could begin in the center and work out to each side. Here, I started on one side and worked across. **C**

4. Pin a second scrap in place. This piece has some interfacing on it, which isn't necessary when you're foundation piecing. If you're working with prints, these fabrics would be placed right sides together. **D**

5. Flip the block over. Sew, using the printed stripes as your guide for the needle or for the edge of the presser foot. Allow at least a ¼" seam allowance. Depending on the width of the stripes you're creating, you may need to trim away excess seam allowance. **E**

6. Press open. Notice that my green strip is a little short. It will just make it into the seam allowance of the finished block, but it's optimal if your strips are longer than the block and can be trimmed later. **F**

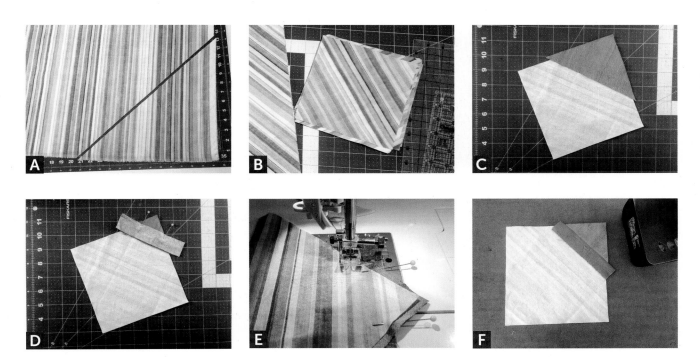

7. Continue to add stripes in the same fashion: Pin, flip the block over, sew along a printed line, and press open. **G** **H**

8. Vary the width of stripes to create interest. **I**

9. Be careful not to create seams too close to the corners and be sure to trim away excess seam allowance here. When you piece the blocks together, you don't want to have too much bulk in the corners. **J** **K** **L**

10. Trim the block down, but follow the 90-degree angle of your ruler, not the edges of the striped fabric. It's possible that the cotton foundation might have warped a little on the bias. **M**

11. A finished block! I chose my stripe widths and colors quite at random. You can get more fussy and selective with color placement and scale if you'd like. **N**

12. I made this grid of nine blocks into a simple pillow cover. **O**

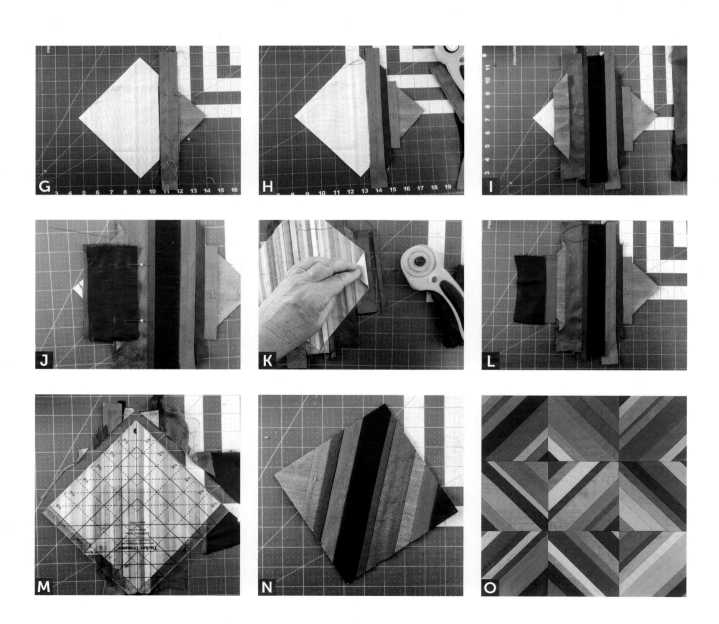

Freestyle Fabric Foundation Piecing

A free-wheeling variation on using striped fabric is to piece onto a foundation with no markings at all. This method should especially appeal to improv and art quilters. The basic principles and benefits of foundation piecing are still present, but precision is not at all the goal.

In this example, I've exploited the bias stretch of strips cut from neckties by curving them a little as I pinned them down. No need to flip the block over; you can sew from the top, following the edge of the fabrics as your guide.

1. Cut bias strips from neckties. Cut a square of cotton foundation fabric in the dimensions of your choice. **A**

2. Position the first strip, manipulating the silk to bend into a nice curve. Here, you can see that I've started in the center and plan to work out to the corners. I could equally have started on one side and worked across. **B**

3. Position the second strip to get an idea of how it will look. Lightweight necktie silks are so easy to shape into curves! **C**

4. Flip the second strip over, right sides together, curving it to follow the edge of piece #1. Pin in place. Sew from the top (no need to flip the block over because there are no sewing lines to follow), allowing a generous ¼″ seam. **D**

5. Press open. **E**

6. Position, flip, pin, sew, and press a third strip into place. **F** **G**

7. Keep adding strips, exploiting that bias stretch to create organic lines and shapes, until the whole foundation is covered. **H**

8. Trim the block. I chose a square, and you can see how the fabric foundation had stretched out of true. You could trim this more loosely into an uneven quadrilateral, maybe HSTs, or even rectangles. **I** **J**

Appliqué Two Ways

I do love a perfect circle! Let me show you how to make one in two different ways, using freezer paper. In traditional appliqué, the circle is sewn on top of the background fabric. In reverse appliqué, the background fabric is cut into a circular frame, and the circle is placed beneath.

For machine appliqué, I like to use Superior Threads' Kimono Silk. It makes appliqué stitches almost invisible. It's a little pricey, so sometimes I use it only as the top thread, with regular sewing thread in a matching color in the bobbin.

Of course, you may want to make a feature of your appliqué stitches. DMC's pearl cotton #8 is my go-to for decorative hand stitching.

BEEF IT UP!

Fusible interfacing is a helpful addition to silk fabrics when employing appliqué techniques. It stabilizes the stretch, stops edges from fraying, and brings opacity to fabrics that are light in weight or color.

More robust silks can still benefit from a misting of starch alternative.

Drawstring Appliqué

1. Cut a circle of freezer paper. With a dry iron, press it *shiny side down* onto the back of a piece of stabilized silk. Freezer paper has a sheer coating of plastic that adheres to fabric when heat is applied. **A**

2. Trim down, leaving a generous ¼″ seam allowance. **B**

3. Thread a needle and knot one end. Stitch with a running stitch all the way around the circle, in the middle of the seam allowance. **C** **D**

4. Gently pull the thread tight, securing the end with a couple of backstitches. **E**

5. Press the fabric so it folds tightly over the edge of the freezer-paper template.

When it looks like a nice, even circle, apply a little steam. **F**

6. Peel off the freezer paper. **G**

7. A perfect circle! **H**

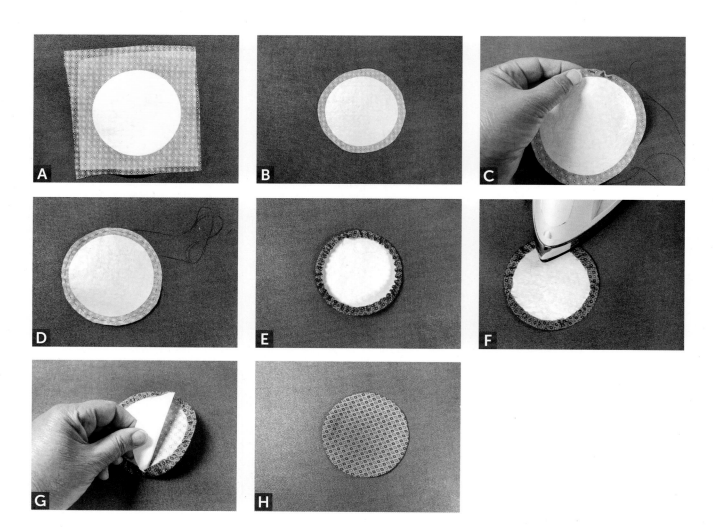

The Rambling Rose Table Runner (page 102) includes circles and leaf shapes. Follow the instructions below to make the leaves.

1. Trace the leaf shape from the Rambling Rose Table Runner Leaf template (page 125) onto freezer paper and cut it out. **A**

2. Press the freezer paper template shiny side down onto the back of the fabric and trim a ¼˝ seam all around. **B**

3. Gather the fabric around the curved part of the leaf, using the drawstring method shown in Drawstring Appliqué (page 60). **C**

4. Press the curved edge and 1 straight side over the edge of the template. **D**

5. Trim away a little seam allowance of the straight edge you just pressed to avoid creating bulk in the tip of the leaf. **E**

6. Press the other straight side of the pointed end of the leaf. Apply a little steam when your fingers are safely out of the way. **F**

7. Trim off the little "ear" sticking out at the tip of the leaf. **G** **H**

8. Carefully peel off the freezer paper template. **I**

9. Press the finished leaf one more time. **J**

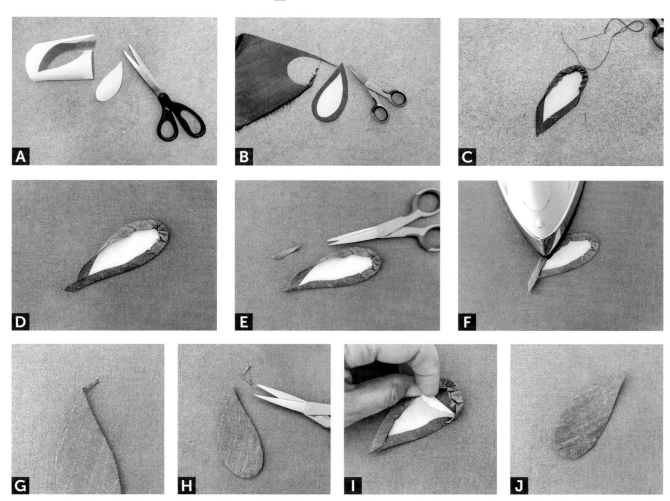

Reverse Appliqué

This technique effectively creates a hole, or a frame, in the background fabric, and another piece of fabric—let's call it "the feature fabric"—is layered underneath.

I learned this *6-Minute Circle* method from quilter Dale Fleming's recorded segment with Alex Anderson. (Sorry, Dale, it takes me a little longer than six minutes!)

1. Press the background fabric nice and flat. Lay it right side down. **A**

2. Cut out a circle the size of your choosing from a sheet of freezer paper. When I want a circle larger than my compasses can draw, I fold my paper into quarters and use my ruler to make a series of dots that join up in a quarter circle curve. If you prefer a more organic "blob" shape, draw freehand. This aperture could be an oval, an egg shape, or any other roughly circular shape. **B C D**

3. Press the freezer paper template shiny side down with a dry iron so it adheres to the back of the background fabric. **E**

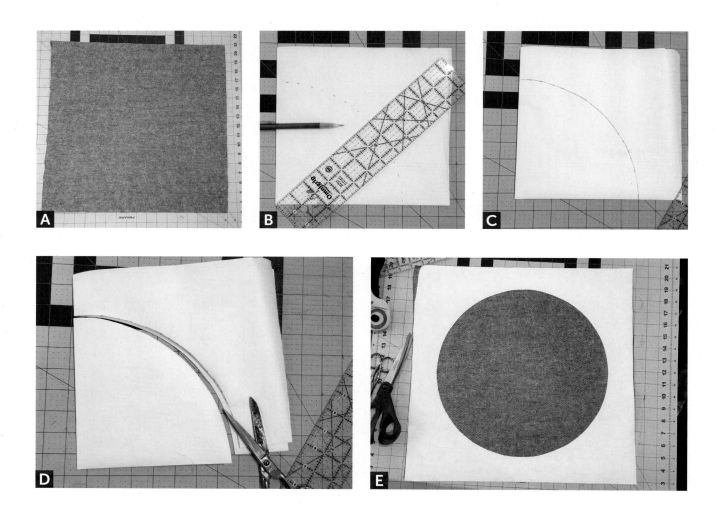

4. Cut out the center of the circle, leaving a ½″ seam allowance. **F**

5. Clip the curved edge approximately every ⅜″, coming to within 1⁄16″ of the paper edge. Tighter curves need more snips than larger ones. **G**

6. Press back the clipped seam allowance, being careful not to scorch your fingertips. **H** **I**

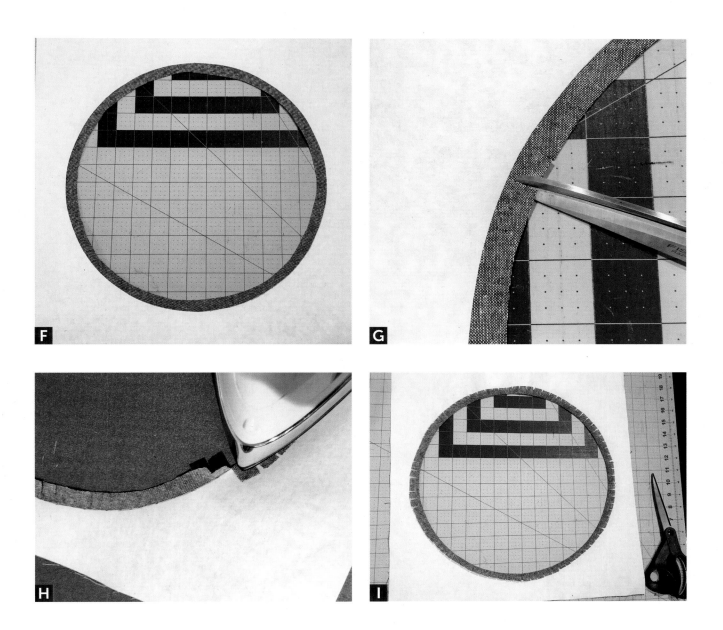

7. You've created a perfectly circular frame! You are about to use glue to baste the two pieces together, but before doing that, take a moment to position the frame exactly as you want it on top of the feature fabric. Here, I am framing a piece of crazy piecing. I'm using pins on the frame and on the crazy piecing to help me line up the 2 pieces quickly when I have wet glue in play. **J**

8. Apply tiny dots of glue to each clipped tab of the seam allowance on the back of the circular frame. White school glue works well, as does Acorn's SeamAlign Gentle Hold Fabric Glue. Note: You are *not* gluing the fabric tabs to the freezer paper—there should be no glue on the freezer paper at all! We are going to peel it off once it has served its purpose. **K**

9. Place the frame glue side down onto the feature fabric, matching up any pins you put in as points of reference. Press firmly and leave to dry for about 5 minutes. **L**

10. When the glue is dry, peel away the freezer-paper frame and set it aside. The freezer paper frame can be used several times before it loses its stick. **M**

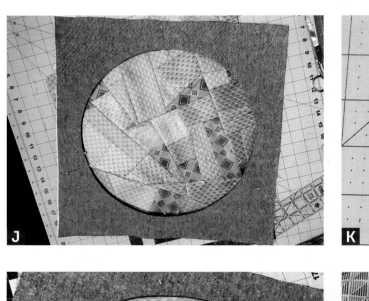

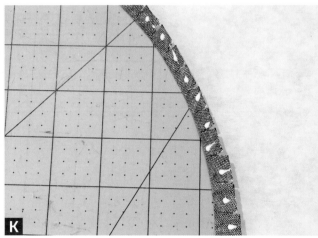

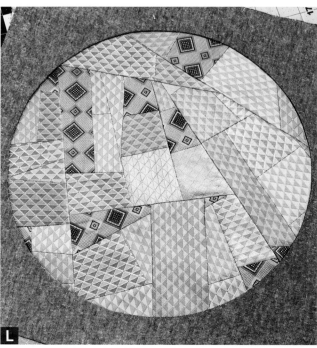

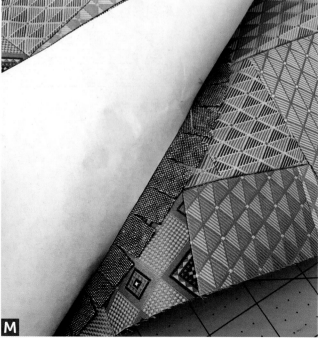

11. With the piece right side up, lift up the frame fabric, and you'll see a sharp crease right next to the clipped edge of the frame.

Stitch a seam exactly in that crease, all around the frame. With tighter curves, a zipper foot can be helpful. **N** **O** **P**

12. Trim away excess feature fabric. **Q**

13. Press once more and admire the beautiful piece of reverse appliqué you've just made. Where's the stitching? It can't be seen! **R**

I have used this reverse-appliqué technique many times and on various scales, and it gives great results every time. Check out an adaptation of this method in the Crazy Circle Pillow (page 74).

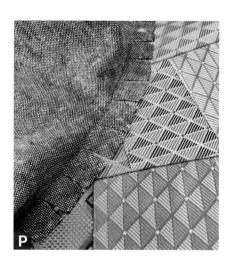

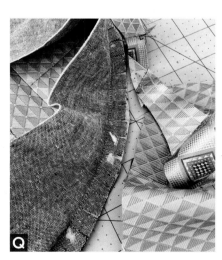

A Word About Fussy Cutting

Many of the techniques and projects in this book provide opportunities for *fussy cutting*, isolating a motif from a printed or woven design and positioning it in a particular way. Fussy cutting is a challenge to your cutting and sewing skills, but it can look so delightfully effective that I think it's worth the trouble.

Using just the Flying Geese block, these four quilt details illustrate just how effective fussy cutting can be in bringing interesting effects to your patchwork designs.

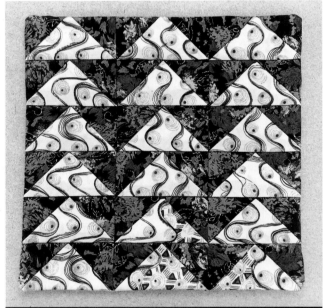

These wavy stripes were fussy cut from a necktie. They bring a vertical direction to the strip of geese without demanding great precision as you position each piece.

This quilt is a good example of something that reads as navy and yellow but contains many shades of each color. I got a kick out of fussy cutting the Lady Liberty print.

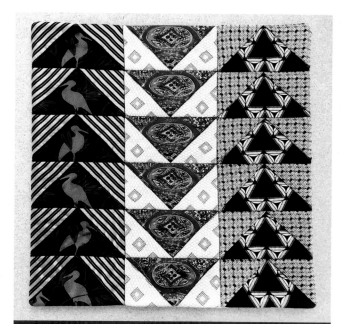

Various motifs have been isolated and cut from printed silks. Notice that not all the birds are identical, but they are all framed within a triangle in a similar way.

Stripes will challenge your pinning skills! Look closely, and you'll see that not every stripe lands completely accurately. It's interesting to me that the eye accepts a certain amount of inaccuracy.

Cut a template from a colored clear plastic binder divider. Don't include seam allowances. I rough cut around the template with a ½˝ seam allowance. These little silk triangles will shape-shift! You get to position them as accurately as possible at the pinning stage. Trace where you want motifs to land with a dry-erase marker. This step allows you to cut multiple pieces with the pattern positioned in the same way.

PROJECTS

The following projects can be copied exactly or simply used for inspiration. Each quilt contains some combination of the techniques outlined in the first portions of this book.

When you're working with reclaimed fabrics, it must be said that it is hard to quote exact fabric requirements. One small quilt I made bears the literal name *Eight Neckties and a Long-Sleeved Shirt.* Another piece, if anyone asks how much fabric was used, elicits the answer "three kimonos."

In all of my quilts, you will see a wide array of fabrics—sometimes creating a scrappy look, and other times reading as one color but, on closer inspection, containing many subtle variations.

Although I favor traditional blocks, I also see myself as an improvisational quilter because every quilt I make is driven by the available fabric. When I run out of a star-player fabric, I have to improvise. These are my options:

1. Stop the quilt right there. Maybe it's a wallhanging or a throw and not the queen size I might have liked.

2. Find a good imitation of that favorite fabric, something that has a similar color scheme and will read the same (from a galloping horse, as they say).

3. Take a new direction with the quilt. Add a whole new border or design element. if you can't make the number of blocks hoped for, add sashing to enlarge your quilt top.

I enjoy the challenge of bringing together a wide array of fabrics and making them cohesive. I get a kick out of harvesting fabric from unwanted and unworn garments or from scraps that have been discarded.

As you approach these projects, be ready with a good stash of silk fabrics and don't be afraid to mix things up a little. Have fun!

Half-Square Triangle Pillow

If you have never pieced silk before, this is a good place to start. All fabrics are fused, which tames the stretch and fray. Depending on what you use for the back of the pillow, you may or may not need to add fusible interfacing to that.

FINISHED PILLOW: 20″ × 20″

Materials

Assorted silks: 4–5 pieces 12″ × 8″ or larger (I used 4 neckties and a 10″ × 10″ piece of Chinese brocade.)

Orange background: Enough to cut 13 squares 4⅞″ × 4⅞″ (I used 1 yard of 14″-wide kimono fabric.) Or ⅓ yard 40″-wide fabric.

Backing: 2 pieces 21″ × 14″ for pillow back

Fusible interfacing: Such as Pellon P44F or similar, 2½ yards

Pillow form: 20″

Cutting

See Stabilize Your Fabrics with Fusible Interfacing, page 24, before cutting.

Assorted silks

Cut 13 squares 4⅞″ × 4⅞″.

Orange background

Cut 13 squares 4⅞″ × 4⅞″.

Backing

Cut 2 rectangles 21″ × 14″ for pillow back.

Construction

MAKE THE PILLOW TOP

1. Pairing up every background square with a square of assorted silks, create 26 HSTs by using the piecing technique in Traditional Machine Piecing with Fused Silks (page 32).

2. For this design, you need only 25 HSTs (you will have 1 left over). Lay them out in a 5 × 5 grid. Find a composition that pleases you. Sew together in vertical strips, as shown.

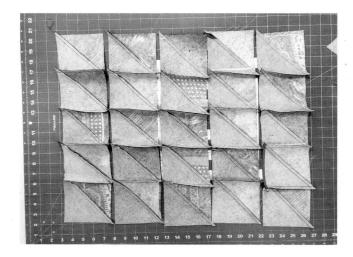

3. Press seams in alternating directions, with 1 strip pressed with seams pointing up and the next strip pressed with seams pointing down. This method will allow you to nest seams.

4. Join strips together. Press seams open.

5. You may choose to quilt this pillow top by machine or by hand before constructing the pillow cover, or leave it unquilted.

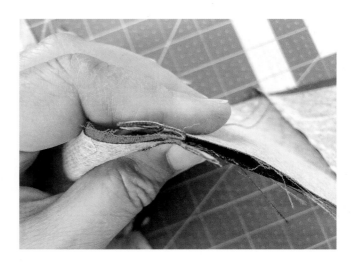

CONSTRUCT THE PILLOW

The easiest method of pillow construction is an envelope closure. I used a silk brocade, which was quite sturdy. If your choice of fabric is stretchy or thin, apply fusible interfacing to give it some support and stability.

1. Sew a ½˝ hem along a 21˝ edge of both backing pieces.

2. Lay the pillow front right side up on your work surface. Place the 2 backing pieces right sides down, overlapping to create an envelope closure. **A** **B**

3. Stitch around all 4 sides of the pillow. **C**

4. Turn right sides out.

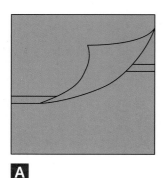

A

B

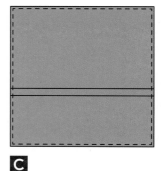

C

Crazy Circle Pillow

This pillow's reverse-appliqué circular frame sets off a small panel of crazy-pieced silk. If you like hand sewing, add some big decorative stitches, or even fancy embroidery stitches, in the style of nineteenth-century crazy quilts.

FINISHED PILLOW: 20˝ × 20˝

Materials

Silk scraps: 8 pieces at least 12˝ × 6˝ each for crazy-pieced center panel.

Beige background: 2/3 yard for pillow front and back (I used a linen and cotton blend.)

Fusible interfacing: for any lightweight fabrics.

Pillow form: 20˝

Freezer paper

Cutting

See Stabilize Your Fabrics with Fusible Interfacing, page 24, before cutting.

Silk scraps

Starting with 8 pieces of silk, create a crazy-pieced center panel, following the directions in Crazy Piecing into Panels (page 33). Your patchwork panel should measure about 15˝ × 15˝ square.

Beige background

Cut a 21˝ × 21˝ square for the pillow front.

Cut 2 pieces 14˝ × 21˝ for the envelope closure on the pillow back.

Construction

1. This pillow features a 14˝ diameter circle. Following the instructions for Reverse Appliqué (page 62), cut a circle from freezer paper, iron it onto the wrong side of the 21˝ square, and continue to follow the instructions to set the crazy-pieced panel into the circular fabric frame.

2. You may choose to quilt this pillow top by machine or by hand before constructing the pillow cover, or leave it unquilted. Shown here is a detail of my big-stitch quilting and machine quilting in simple echoes around the circle

3. To finish the pillow, follow the instructions to Construct the Pillow (page 72) for the Half-Square Triangle Pillow.

CRAZY HEART PILLOW

The heart shape requires that we stitch the seam from the front of the piece, more in the style of traditional appliqué, instead of sewing in the crease.

Follow the instructions in the main project to build a crazy-pieced panel.

Construction

1. Using the Crazy Heart Frame template (page 125), cut a heart-shaped frame in the center of the freezer paper and fuse it to the wrong side of the pillow-front fabric.

2. Follow Steps 1–10 of the Reverse Appliqué technique (page 62).

3. The heart-shaped frame should be appliquéd from the front. Use a narrow buttonhole stitch and a fine silk thread if you want your stitches to disappear. Use pearl cotton and large embroidery stitches if you want to make a feature of this area.

4. You may choose to quilt this pillow top by machine or by hand before constructing the pillow cover, or leave it unquilted.

5. To finish the pillow, follow the instructions to Construct the Pillow (page 72) for the Half-Square Triangle Pillow.

Mothers and Daughters Bed Runner

Measuring 88˝ × 40˝, this quilt drapes across the end of a bed. A great vehicle for using small scraps of silk, for combining all kinds of textiles, and for playing with light and dark values, it's a really versatile design.

This quilt is a souvenir of the year my two daughters left home. It includes one large mama goose for every two little ones—hence the name.

This quilt includes 2,508 pieces. That number sounds excessive when I see it written down, but really, this quilt wasn't hard to make. I built it gradually, just choosing two colors at a time that looked good together. If you take a look at a line of geese, you may notice that the colors of the geese shift from brown to red to blue to green, but that's about as much planning as went into my color choices. Construct it in several strips at a time so you can pin a dozen pieces, sew a dozen seams, and press a dozen times for efficiency.

FINISHED RUNNER: 88˝ × 40˝

Materials

Dark-value silk scraps: Scraps, neckties, clothing, and anything else you can find. I used more than 80 neckties in this quilt. If you have fewer neckties, augment your stash with a yard of dupioni silk or a silk garment that will yield plenty of fabric. My design is totally scrappy. Yours could include as few as 2 colors. You'll need 40 neckties or the equivalent number of 12˝ × 8˝ or larger pieces, **or** 3 yards 40˝-wide fabric.

Light-value silk scraps: As with the dark-value scraps, you'll need a variety of silk fabric scraps, approximately 40 neckties or the equivalent number of 12˝ × 8˝ or larger pieces, **or** 3 yards 40˝-wide fabric.

Foundation: 4 yards 45˝-wide lightweight cotton muslin *or* 2 yards 90˝ or wider lightweight cotton muslin if drafting your own foundations

or

Foundation By The Yard Flying Geese, 3 panels

or

EZ Piecing Flying Geese 2˝ × 4˝, 3 packs, *and* EZ Piecing Flying Geese 1˝ × 2˝, 2 packs

Large Flying Geese Strips Foundation template (page 122)

Small Flying Geese Strips Foundation template (page 122)

Cutting

Cut 154 squares 4½″ × 4½″ for the 2″ × 4″ Flying Geese Blocks.

Subcut these squares diagonally to make 308 goose triangles.

Cut 528 squares 2″ × 2″ for the 1″ × 2″ Flying Geese Blocks.

Subcut these squares diagonally to make 1,056 background triangles.

Cut 308 squares 3½″ × 3½″ for the 2″ × 4″ Flying Geese Blocks.

Subcut these squares diagonally to make 616 background triangles.

Cut 264 squares 2½″ × 2½″ for the 1″ × 2″ Flying Geese Blocks.

Subcut these squares diagonally to make 528 goose triangles.

Construction

1. Piece onto strips of fabric foundation of your choice, drafted or preprinted (see Traditional Fabric Foundation Piecing, page 37).

7 strips of large geese (A): 44 units each

6 strips of small geese (B): 88 units each

2. Lay strips in alternating columns (A, B, A, B, and so forth), starting and ending with an A strip. **A**

3. Sew strips together and press these seams open. **B**

4. Quilt and bind as desired.

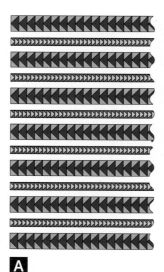

A

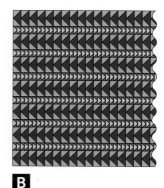

B

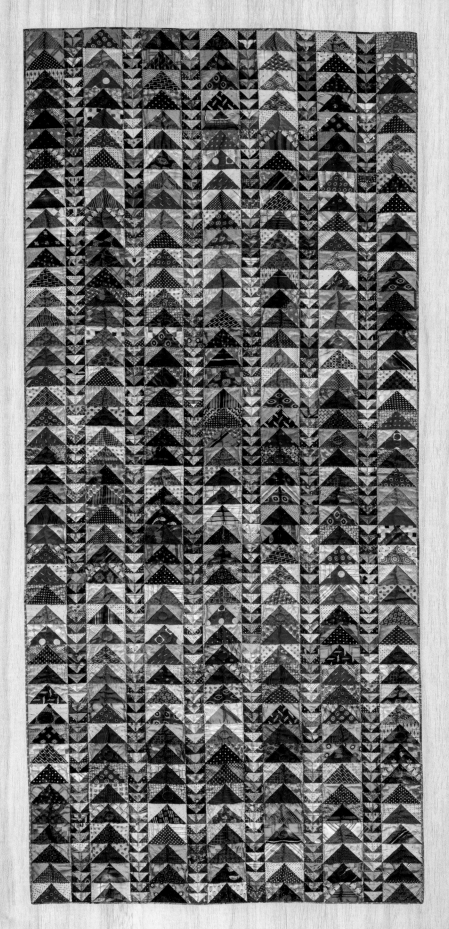

Geese Crossing Mini Quilt

Combining crazy-pieced panels with strips of Flying Geese, this 20˝ mini quilt can be completed in a day. This is the sample for a workshop I love to teach. The crazy piecing is a loose, improvisational experience, while the Flying Geese are all about precision and accurate drafting and stitching.

Before you sew your block together, experiment with layout variations; the geese can fly into the center or out to the edge of the block.

Shown here as a mini quilt, your Geese Crossing patchwork could instead be finished as a decorative pillow or a gorgeous panel on the back of a jacket.

FINISHED QUILT: 20˝ × 20˝

Materials

Silk scraps: 8–10 neckties or equivalent number of 12˝ × 8˝ pieces of silk

Contrasting silk: ¼ yard for Flying Geese backgrounds

Fusible interfacing: 1 yard fusible interfacing for the lighter-weight silks in your selection

Foundation: ¼ yard lightweight muslin if drafting your own foundations

or ⸺⸺⸺⸺⸺⸺⸺⸺⸺⸺

Foundation by the Yard Flying Geese

or ⸺⸺⸺⸺⸺⸺⸺⸺⸺⸺⸺⸺

EZ Piecing Flying Geese Strips

Large Flying Geese Strips Foundation template (page 122)

Cutting

See Stabilize Your Fabrics with Fusible Interfacing, page 24, before cutting.

Silk scraps

Cut 8 squares 4½˝.

Subcut these squares diagonally to make 16 triangles. (Set these aside and use the rest of the silk for the crazy piecing.)

Crazy-pieced fabric

Cut 4 squares 9˝ × 9˝ for the 4 quadrants and 1 square 5˝ × 5˝ for the center from the crazy-pieced fabric you make (see Crazy Piecing into Panels, page 33).

Contrasting silk

Cut 16 squares 3½˝ × 3½˝.

Subcut these squares diagonally to make 32 triangles.

Lightweight muslin

Cut 4 rectangles 5½˝ × 9½˝ for fabric foundations if drafting your own.

Quilted by the author

Construction

Use ½˝ seams throughout.

1. On the muslin rectangles, draft 4 foundation strips of Large Flying Geese Strips Foundation as shown in Traditional Fabric Foundation Piecing (page 37) *or* trace the Large Flying Geese Strips Foundation templates (page 122). You can also use Benartex's preprinted Foundation By The Yard or EZ Piecing Flying Geese Strips for the construction.

2. Piece the cut triangles onto the strip, completing 4 strips of 4 geese, each trimmed and measuring 5˝ × 9˝ unfinished.

3. Construct a large-enough crazy-pieced panel (see Crazy Piecing Into Panels, page 33) to yield 4 squares 9˝ × 9˝ for the 4 quadrants and 1 square 5˝ × 5˝ for the center.

4. Bring these components together as shown in the diagram. **A**

5. Attach a crazy-pieced 9˝ square on either side of a strip of geese. Repeat with the other 2 crazy-pieced squares. Attach the 5˝ end of 2 Flying Geese strips to either side of the 5˝ center square. Seam all 3 components together as shown. **B**

6. Bring the whole piece together with the final 3 seams. **C**

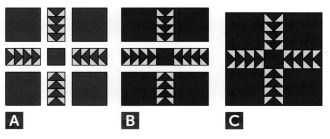

A   **B**   **C**

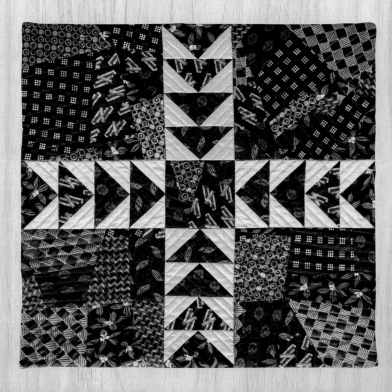

DIAGONAL VARIATION

A variation on this piece sets the Flying Geese on the diagonal and finishes at 17˝ × 17˝.

Quilted by the author

For this orientation, follow the materials and cutting instructions in the main project. To begin construction, complete Steps 1–3 of the main project. Next, cut the crazy pieced panel as follows:

1. Cut 2 squares 10˝ × 10˝.

2. Subcut these squares diagonally to make a total of 4 triangles for the sides.

3. Cut 1 square 5˝ × 5˝ for the center.

4. Cut 2 squares 4½˝ × 4½˝.

5. Subcut the 4½˝ × 4½˝ squares diagonally to make a total of 4 triangles for the corners.

6. Lay the pieces out as shown in the diagram. **A**

7. Attach the short sides of the side triangles to either side of the long sides of 2 Flying Geese strips. Attach the short sides of the remaining Flying Geese strips to the 5˝ center square. **B**

8. Bring the 3 sections together with 2 long seams. **C**

9. Add the corner triangles last. **D**

10. Quilt and bind or face as desired.

A

B

C

D

Every Which Way

You can see how this quilt has its origins in the *Geese Crossing Mini Quilt* (page 82). My color palette for this quilt was inspired by San Francisco Bay sunsets. I encourage you to choose your own palette based on what inspires you or simply by what's in your stash. I gathered together many neckties, design-room swatches, and kimonos that fit my color theme. Notice the dark dupioni silk that appears throughout the background of the Flying Geese strips? These are actually two colors used randomly, a purple and a dark red.

I kept the lightest colors for the geese and fussy cut some favorite motifs for the circles at each of the 25 intersections.

FINISHED QUILT: 68˝ × 68˝

Materials

Crazy-pieced fabric: Gather enough sunset colors to create *a lot* of crazy-pieced panels. A stash of 70–80 neckties or the equivalent number of 12˝ × 8˝ or larger pieces of rescued fabrics will be enough.

Light-colored silk scraps (A): Approximately 2½ yards for the Flying Geese

Dark solid-colored silk (B): 4½ yards dupioni or any solid-colored silk for the borders, binding, and Flying Geese backgrounds

Foundation: 2½ yards lightweight muslin if drafting your own foundations

or --

Foundation by the Yard Flying Geese, 3 panels (you will use only the 2˝ × 4˝ geese for this project)

or --

EZ Piecing Flying Geese 2˝ × 4˝, 2 packs

Freezer paper

Fusible interfacing

Cutting

See Stabilize Your Fabrics with Fusible Interfacing, page 24, before cutting.

Crazy-pieced panels

Build multiple panels of crazy-pieced fabric until they are large enough for you to cut 3 or 4 squares 9˝ × 9˝ from them. Keep all the scraps and keep joining them together. Some squares will feature smaller patches than others. That's fine.

Cut a total of 36 squares 9˝ × 9˝ from the crazy-pieced fabric.

Flying Geese

Cut 120 squares 4½˝ × 4½˝ from the light-colored silk scraps (A).

  Subcut these squares diagonally to make 240 triangles.

Cut 240 squares 3½˝ × 3½˝ from the dark solid-colored silk (B).

  Subcut these squares diagonally to make 480 triangles.

Cutting continued on page 88.

Quilted by
Nancy Williams

Cutting continued.

25 center squares

Cut 12 squares 5″ × 5″ from the light-colored silk scraps (A).

Cut 13 squares 5″ × 5″ from the dark solid-colored silk (B).

Cut 13 circles with a 3″ diameter from the light-colored silk scraps (A).

Cut 12 circles with a 3″ diameter from the dark solid-colored silk (B).

HSTs in the border

Cut 68 squares 2⅞″ × 2⅞″ from from the light-colored silk scraps (A) *with fusible interfacing added.*

Cut 68 squares 2⅞″ × 2⅞″ from the dark solid-colored silk (B) *with fusible interfacing added.*

Corners

Cut 4 squares 2½″ from the dark solid-colored silk (B) *with fusible interfacing added.*

Foundation

Cut 60 strips 5½″ × 9½″ from the lightweight muslin if drafting your own foundations.

Construction

1. Complete 60 strips of 4 Flying Geese using the triangles cut from fabric A for the geese and fabric B for the background (see Traditional Fabric Foundation Piecing, page 37).

2. Using freezer-paper templates, appliqué (or reverse appliqué) a fussy-cut circle with a 2¼″ diameter into the center of each 5″ × 5″ square (see Appliqué Two Ways, page 59). Sew light circles on dark squares and dark circles on light squares.

3. Pair light and dark 2⅞″ × 2⅞″ squares. Make 136 HSTs for the border (see Traditional Machine Piecing with Fused Silks, page 32). In the border, with the addition of fusible interfacing, use ¼″ seams.

4. Piece the HSTs into 4 border strips containing 34 HSTs each. Note the orientation of light and dark triangles in the illustration in Step 5.

A design wall is super-helpful at this stage. Lay out all the blocks in the composition shown in the diagram. You'll notice in my quilt that the crazy-pieced blocks with small pieces are in the center of the quilt, and those closer to the edges have larger pieces. I have also exploited any slight diagonal lines in the crazy blocks by positioning them so they radiate out from the center.

Take some time to make sure that colors are evenly distributed across the quilt. Take photos as you change things around and see whether anything jumps out at you that needs to be switched around.

Make sure that the geese are flying in alternating directions, *Every Which Way!* (Thanks to my friend Kirsten for naming this quilt!)

5. Assemble the quilt top in columns, as shown in the diagram. Sew the blocks together in columns using ½″ seams. Add a border strip across the top and bottom. Add a 2½″ square of fabric B to each end of the remaining 2 borders. Attach borders to each side as shown. **A**

6. Quilt and bind as desired.

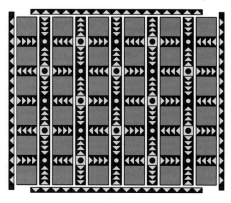

A

Kaleidoscope Pineapple

The trick to this nine-block quilt is all in the fabric choices. I had a big box of striped neckties that I had been hesitant to use because those big, bold stripes have such strong visual impact.

The Kaleidoscope Pineapple Coloring Page (page 126) is for you to photocopy or download and print and play with. Reach for your colored pencils and take some time to explore the effects of color placement. If you prefer to use computer-based design tools, do so.

Although this quilt has only nine blocks, it includes 16 color groupings, each containing five fabrics. Yes! You could use 80 different fabrics in this pineapple quilt! (But feel free to simplify.)

The diagonal X motifs are formed when four blocks join. The pieces that are actually the corners of the blocks become the visual centers of the colored Xs. Planning is key! Color your design sheet; mark color placement on your fabric foundation blocks, if that helps; and lay your fabric strips on trays to stay organized.

I chose a silver-gray jacquard silk fabric for all the center squares of each block. It's interesting how many people have commented on how much they like those squares!

The background and border is a black silk and rayon textile with a subtle, dark navy chrysanthemum motif. It has a matte finish, which sets off the shine of the necktie silks beautifully. In my quilt, I added 5″ finished borders. Yours could be narrower, wider, or more decorative.

FINISHED QUILT: 40″ × 40″

Materials

Dark background (B): 2 yards 44″-wide fabric for the dark background and border

Foundation: 1 yard lightweight muslin if drafting your own foundations

9 Pineapple Kaleidoscope by Julia McLeod fabric foundation blocks by EZ Piecing

or

Kaleidoscope Pineapple Pineapple Corner Triangle template (page 120)

Assorted silks: 80 pieces 7″ × 8″. You can use up to 80 different silk fabrics. The most you will need of any single fabric is about 7″ × 8″, but note that fussy cutting, while delightfully effective, is wasteful. The majority of these silks came from neckties.

Quilted by the author

Cutting

Dark background (B)

Cut 4 rectangles 6″ × 42″ for borders.

Cut 18 strips 2″ × width of fabric

Lightweight muslin

Cut 9 squares 11″ × 11″ for fabric foundations if drafting your own.

Assorted silks

For Rounds 3–9 of the block, fussy cut strips 2″ wide so that the line of the stripes in the fabric run perpendicular to the edges of the strip. This method gives you ½″ seam allowances. You could cut strips a little narrower (1¾″) if you need to skimp on fabric, see A Word About Fussy Cutting (page 66) for helpfulf tips on fussy cutting. Exact dimensions for each round of this Pineapple block can be found in the Pineapple Block Cutting Instructions table (page 45).

For the corner fabrics of each block (Round 10), cut 4 triangles.

For fussy cutting corner triangles, cut a template out of clear, lightweight plastic (use an old binder divider). Trace the Kaleidoscope Pineapple Pineapple Corner Triangle template (page 120). Cut ½″ from the edges of the template.

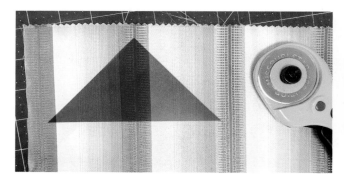 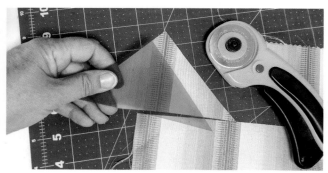

Construction

1. According to your color plan or the finished quilt image, piece each Pineapple block by following the instructions in Piecing the Pineapple Block (page 45). Trim the block, leaving ½″ seam allowances.

2. Arrange the blocks in a grid of 9, sew them into 3 columns, and then join the columns together.

3. Attach a border strip to each side. Miter the corners. Press.

4. Quilt and bind as desired.

PINEAPPLE VARIATIONS
Note that not all Pineapple blocks are the same. This one, finishing at 10″ square, has a center, four "blades," and a corner triangle. Other Pineapple blocks may have more or fewer blades.

TAKE TWO!

I enjoyed making this pineapple quilt so much that I made a second one. This time, I used a light-colored background fabric and the pineapples were dark—many shades of green. The color-wash effect took a little planning but wasn't as complicated as arranging all the stripes for the *Kaleidoscope Pineapple* quilt. The border is pieced in stripes rather than solid, and the quilting, by Kathy Ritter, is significantly fancier.

Quilted by Kathy Ritter

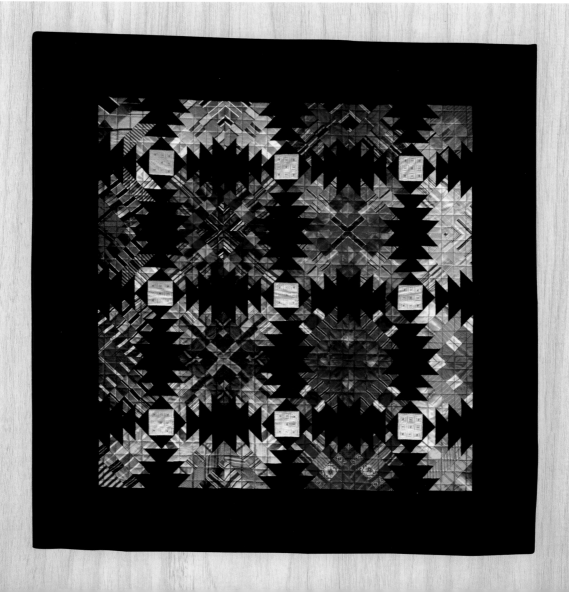

Flying Circus

This small quilt combines traditional piecing, fabric foundation–pieced Flying Geese and Grandmother's Fan blocks, and a fussy-cut appliqué circle at the center of each. The entire set of foundations is available from EZ Piecing, but you can also draft it yourself by tracing the provided foundation templates or by using Benartex's Foundation by the Yard Flying Geese and Grandmother's Fans.

For this piece, I cut from a length of silk tie fabric, a polyester floral blouse, a piece of kimono lining, and some scraps of red dupioni silk. Allow for the fact that fussy cutting is a little wasteful because the motifs you cut out can be spaced quite far apart. The rest of the fabric can be used for other, scrappier projects. To appliqué the center circle, I used Superior Threads' 100 wt. 2-ply filament Kimono Silk in a very narrow buttonhole stitch.

Thanks to my Facebook follower Rebecca Blair, who came up with the name for this pattern. Anyone else a *Monty Python* fan?

FINISHED QUILT: 24˝ × 24˝

Materials

Red stripe: ¼ yard

Pink floral: ½ yard to allow for good fussy-cutting choices

Light pink/cream: ¼ yard

Red: ¼ yard *or* scraps

Foundation: 6˝ × width of fabric from lightweight muslin if drafting your own foundations

or --

Foundation by the Yard Flying Geese and Grandmother's Fan, by Benartex (From 1 panel of each design, cut 4 fans and 8 sections of 2 geese each.)

or --

EZ Piecing's Flying Circus Foundation Kit

Grandmother's Fan Foundation template (pages 120–121)

Cutting

See Stabilize Your Fabrics with Fusible Interfacing, page 24, before cutting.

Red stripe

Cut 12 fan blades, fussy cut if desired, using the Grandmother's Fan Foundation template.

Cut 8 squares 5˝ × 5˝ with fusible interfacing attached, if needed.

Pink floral

Cut 12 fan blades, fussy cut if desired.

Fussy cut 4 squares 5˝ × 5˝ with fusible interfacing attached, if needed.

Fussy cut 1 circle with a 5˝ diameter with fusible interfacing attached, if needed.

Light pink/cream

Cutting continued on page 96.

Quilted by the author

Cutting continued.

Cut 4 Grandmother's Fan Foundation Part B for the foundation-pieced Fan blocks.

Cut 8 squares 4½″ × 4½″.

Subcut these squares diagonally to yield 16 goose triangles.

Red

Cut 16 squares 3½″ × 3½″.

Subcut these squares diagonally to yield 32 background triangles.

Construction

1. Piece 4 Fan blocks, following the step-by-step instructions in Piecing Grandmother's Fan (page 49), but *without adding the center quarter circle.*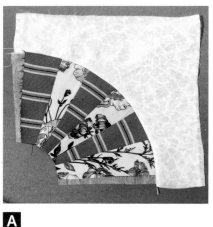

Join the 4 blocks together to make a circle with a hole in the center.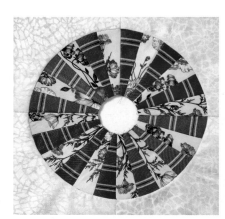

2. From freezer paper, cut 1 circle with a 4″ diameter. Fuse the freezer-paper circle to a fussy-cut circle of pink floral fabric. Use the Drawstring Appliqué method (page 60) to turn raw edges under.

3. Position the center circle with dots of glue.

4. Appliqué the circle to the center of the circle of fans with a straight, zigzag, or buttonhole stitch. I chose Superior Thread's Kimono Silk thread. Fine thread disappears into the patchwork. Thicker thread makes a feature out of your stitches.

5. From the back, remove the circular freezer-paper template.

6. Trim the center block to measure 16½″.

A

B

C

D

E

F

7. Trace 8 Flying Circus 2-Geese Strips Foundation templates (page 123) or cut pairs of geese from Foundation by the Yard or the EZ Piecing foundation. Piece these blocks following step-by-step instructions for Flying Geese in Traditional Fabric Foundation Piecing (page 37).

8. Sew together Flying Geese blocks, red striped squares, and pink fussy-cut floral squares as shown.

9. Sew borders on the top and bottom and then along sides. Press seams open toward the center of the block.

This digital mockup shows how fun a quilt would look if we made *Flying Circus* nine times. **H**

10. Quilt and bind as desired.

Stars Aligned

Once again, Flying Geese and Grandmother's Fan blocks come together, but in this design, the geese fly through the middle of nine large circles of dark blue fans, creating bright stars where they meet. The stars appear to glow because three shades of orange are in the background of the Flying Geese strips, going from light to dark. A lively cotton print dances in the background.

FINISHED QUILT: 72″ × 72″

Materials

Background (A): 2½ yards printed cotton or silk

Dark blue silk scraps (B): 35 neckties or equivalent number of 12″ × 8″ pieces of silk for fan blades

Light blue silk scraps (C): 20 neckties or equivalent number of 12″ × 8″ pieces of silk for border and geese

White dupioni silk (D): ½ yard 44″-wide fabric

Red dupioni silk (E): ½ yard 44″-wide fabric

Peach silk (F): Enough for 36 squares 3½″ × 3½″, or ½ yard 44″-wide fabric

Orange silk (G): Enough for 36 squares 3½″ × 3½″, or ½ yard 44″-wide fabric

Dark orange silk (H): Enough for 36 squares 3½″ × 3½″, or ½ yard 44″-wide fabric

Rust silk (I): Enough for 36 squares 3″ × 3″, or ½ yard 44″-wide fabric for the fan centers

Foundation: 4 yards lightweight muslin if drafting your own foundations (see Using Muslin, below)

Grandmother's Fan Foundation template (pages 120–121)

Large Flying Geese Strips Foundation template (page 122)

or ---

Grandmother's Fan Foundation by the Yard: 3 panels *and*

Flying Geese Foundation by the Yard: 2 panels

You will need to draft the border separately by tracing the Stars Aligned Border Foundation template (page 124).

or ---

EZ Piecing Stars Aligned Foundation Kit

USING MUSLIN: If you plan to draft your own foundations, you will need 4 yards of lightweight muslin, as indicated in the Materials List. Following the illustration, trace the Grandmother's Fan Foundation template 36 times, the Large Flying Geese Strips Foundation 36 times, and the Stars Aligned Border Foundation template 4 times.

Border strip made with fabrics A and C.

Quilted by
Nancy Williams

Cutting

See Stabilize Your Fabrics with Fusible Interfacing, page 24, before cutting.

Background print (A)

Cut 36 shoulder sections for Grandmother's Fan blocks by using the Grandmother's Fan Foundation template (page 120–121).

Cut 6 squares 4½″ × 4½″.

 Subcut these squares diagonally to make 12 Flying Geese triangles.

Cut 52 border triangles. Use the Stars Aligned Border Triangle Patch template (page 123).

Dark blue silk scraps (B)

Cut 216 fan blades by using the Grandmother's Fan Blade template (page 121).

Light blue silk scraps (C)

Cut 56 triangles by using the Stars Aligned Border Triangle Patch template (page 123).

Cut 12 squares 4½″ × 4½″.

 Subcut these squares diagonally to make 24 Flying Geese triangles.

White dupioni silk (D)

Cut 36 squares 3½″ × 3½″.

 Subcut these squares diagonally to make 72 Flying Geese background triangles.

Add fusible interfacing to the remaining white dupioni silk. Cut 9 squares 5″ × 5″.

Red dupioni silk (E)

Cut 54 squares 4½″ × 4½″.

 Subcut these squares diagonally to make 108 Flying Geese triangles.

Peach silk (F)

Cut 36 squares 3½″ × 3½″.

 Subcut these squares diagonally to make 72 Flying Geese background triangles.

Orange silk (G)

Cut 36 squares 3½″ × 3½″.

 Subcut these squares diagonally to make 72 Flying Geese background triangles.

Dark orange silk (H)

Cut 36 squares 3½″ × 3½″.

 Subcut these squares in half diagonally to make 72 Flying Geese background triangles.

Rust silk (I)

Cut 36 quarter circles using Part B of the Grandmother's Fan Foundation template (page 121).

Construction

1. Following the instructions in Piecing Grandmother's Fan (page 49), foundation piece 36 blocks.

2. Following the quilt layout diagram, foundation piece 36 strips of 4 Flying Geese, following the instructions in Traditional Fabric Foundation Piecing (page 37).

Quilt layout diagram

The first goose will be fabric C in 24 strips. Note also the position of the background triangle colors H, G, F, and D—a gradation from orange to white. This use of color is what makes the stars "glow" at the center of each circle.

The first goose will be fabric A in 12 strips.

3. Connect the Grandmother's Fan, Flying Geese, and center-square blocks into sections and columns as shown. Make sure to check the position of the geese made from fabric A—they will be positioned around the outside of the quilt, while the lighter blue geese made from fabric C will meet in the body of the quilt to form 12 blue squares. Sew the columns together.

4. Piece the border strips onto the fabric foundations. Attach the borders to all 4 sides, mitering the corners.

5. Quilt and bind as desired.

Rambling Rose Table Runner

This small project requires all the techniques demonstrated in this book.

Bands of strip-pieced silks are joined at each end by foundation-pieced fans. A border of HSTs runs around the outer edge, while appliquéd roses and leaves wind down the center. Expertly quilted by Sue Fox, this piece looks good as a wallhanging or a table topper. You can lengthen or shorten it in increments of 2½″, to keep the border pattern consistent.

My tip is to construct the HST borders first and then trim the length of the center panel to match. Everyone's ¼″ seam allowance is a little different; your final measurements may vary.

The diagram, right, shows how all the components come together.

FINISHED RUNNER: 23½″ × 43½″

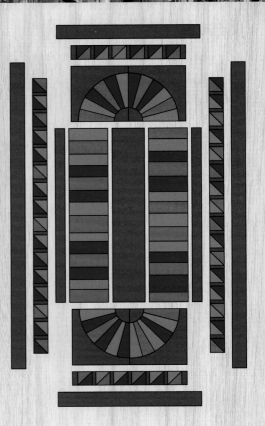

Materials

Background dupioni silk: 1 yard *with fusible interfacing applied*

Silk scraps: Approximately 1 yard for striped bands, Grandmother's Fans, and HSTs

Pink and orange silk scraps: Approximately ¼ yard for roses

Green and brown silk scraps: 20 pieces 5″ × 2½″ for leaves

Freezer paper

Striped cotton print: ⅓ yard for striped center band foundations

Bias tape or ribbon: ½″-wide for stem

Foundation: Lightweight muslin if drafting your own Grandmother's Fan foundations

or ---

Foundation by the Yard Grandmother's Fan, 1 panel

Grandmother's Fan Foundation template (pages 120–121)

> ### ▌ BIAS TAPE ▌
> I used a bias-tape maker to make the curved stem. Spray your fabric with a little starch alternative before pulling it through the tape maker. This step will help it keep a crease until you're ready to appliqué with it.

Quilted by
Sue Fox

Cutting

See Stabilize Your Fabrics with Fusible Interfacing, page 24, before cutting.

Background dupioni silk

Center strip: Cut 1 strip 4½˝ × 25˝.

Side strips: Cut 2 strips 1½˝ × 25˝.

Outer border: Cut 2 strips 2˝ × 20˝ for each end; cut 2 strips 2˝ × 44˝ for the long sides.

Sashing between HSTs: Cut 1 long strip 1˝ wide and 115˝ long.

Grandmother's Fan blocks: Cut 4 Part B and 4 Part C.

Silk scraps

HSTs: Cut 44 squares 2⅞˝ × 2⅞˝.

Grandmother's Fan blades: Cut 24.

Striped center bands: Cut multiple 6˝ strips in varying widths.

Pink and orange silk scraps

4˝ diameter circles: Cut 9.

2½˝ diameter circles: Cut 9.

Green and brown silk scraps

Rambling Rose Table Runner Leaf: Cut 20.

Freezer paper

Rambling Rose Table Runner 3½˝ Diameter Appliqué Circle: Cut several. Freezer-paper templates can be reused.

Rambling Rose Table Runner 2˝ Diameter Appliqué Circle: Cut several. Freezer-paper templates can be reused.

Rambling Rose Table Runner Leaf: Cut several, tracing the pattern (page 125). Freezer-paper templates can be reused.

Striped cotton print

Striped center bands: Cut 2 strips 27˝ × 6˝ for foundations.

Construction

1. Begin with the HSTs. Pair the 2⅞˝ squares randomly to make 44 HSTs, following the method in Traditional Machine Piecing with Fused Silks (page 32).

2. With the sashing in 1 long strip, sew 42 of the HSTs, right sides together, to the sashing strip. Cut them apart and press seams toward sashing.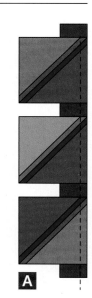

3. Join the sashed HSTs into 4 units: 2 rows of 6 and 2 rows of 15. Add a piece of sashing onto the end of each of the short rows. Add 1 HST onto one end of each of the long rows. Measure the length of the 2 short HST borders. They should measure 15½˝. Some variation is to be expected.

4. Piece 4 Grandmother's Fan blocks. Join them together in 2 semicircles. Check the length of your short borders. Trim the double Fan blocks to that size. See the diagram.

5. Match the center seam of the 2 blocks to the center of the HST border. Pin and sew the semicircular Fan blocks to the short HST borders with a ¼˝ seam.

6. Using the strips of striped printed cotton as foundations, and following the instructions in Using Striped Fabrics as Foundations (page 54), piece 2 bands of irregular stripes.

7. Sew the finished strip-pieced bands on either side of the center strip of background fabric. Add the side strips of background fabric to the outer edges, creating the center panel.

8. Now, take a look at the measurements of all your components. Trim the center panel, if necessary, so that when it is sewn to the semicircular fans, the HST border fits along each long side.

9. Attach the semicircular fans to the top and bottom of the center panel. Add the side strips of half square triangles to the sides of the center panel.

10. Attach the 2˝ wide outer border to the top, bottom, and sides of your piece.

11. Appliqué a winding stem down the center of the quilt. Mine is ½˝ wide and was made with a bias-tape maker.

12. Following the instructions for Drawstring Appliqué (page 60), make 9 large and 9 small circles by using the Rambling Rose Table Runner 2˝ Diameter Appliqué Circle and Rambling Rose Table Runner 3½˝ Diameter Appliqué Circle templates (page 125). One rose is made up of a small circle on top of a larger one, set a little off-center. **B**

B

13. If you want to copy my design exactly, make 20 leaves by using the Rambling Rose Table Runner Leaf template (page 125).

14. Arrange the leaves and flowers as you like and sew them down. Notice that I have the pointy end of the leaves attached to the stem, but the round end of the leaves attached to the roses in the corners.

15. Quilt and bind as desired. It's worth noting Sue Fox's beautiful quilting on this piece. She used neon-colored 40-wt 2-ply high-tenacity Magnifico thread by Superior Threads to brighten a slightly dull color palette.

Gallery

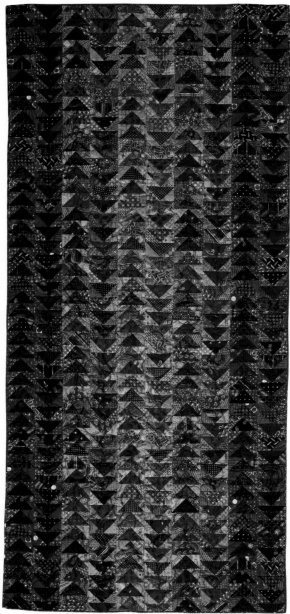

BLAZE, 40˝ × 80˝, pieced by Julia McLeod, machine quilted by Sue Fox

Blaze is a bed runner made from columns of 2˝ × 4˝ fabric foundation-pieced Flying Geese. When collecting neckties, you'll notice that red is a really popular color! Fortunately, red is a favorite of mine. I drew from four piles of neckties, grouped by color: dark red, bright red, orange, and gold.

SALT POINT, 40˝ × 88˝, pieced by Julia McLeod, machine quilted by Sue Fox

Salt Point is the third Flying Geese bed runner I made. This time, the rows of 2˝ × 4˝ geese fly across the width of the quilt. I made ten piles of neckties graded from white through shades of gray to black. If you look carefully, you'll see how each row starts with a white goose on a black background and ends with a black goose on a white background.

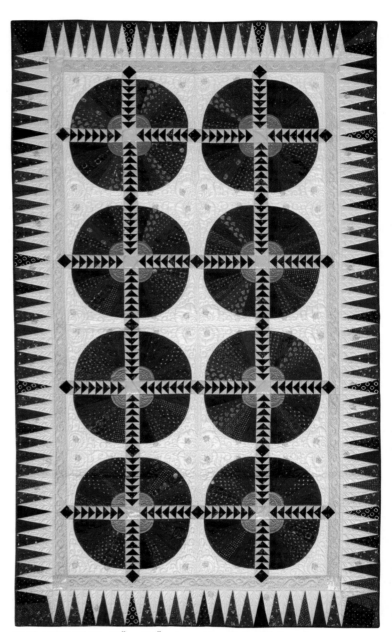

SUNDAY BEST, 40″ × 88″, pieced by Julia McLeod, machine quilted by Sue Fox

Sunday Best uses pairs of fabric foundation-pieced geese in a block known as Wild Goose Chase or Dutchman's Puzzle. When I visit family in the UK, I always search thrift shops for neckties. It's noticeable that British men are more willing to wear pastel colors. Look at all the pinks, lilacs, pale yellows, and mint greens in this quilt!

SARI NOT SARI, 48″ × 84″, pieced by Julia McLeod, machine quilted by Sue Fox

Sari Not Sari is a cousin quilt of *Stars Aligned* (page 98). I used many red and black neckties, a cream sari and its gold border, and small squares from a gold lamé Japanese sash, known as an *obi*.

GULABI, 41″ × 41″,
pieced by Julia McLeod,
machine quilted by Sue Fox

Gulabi is the Hindu word for "pink." I found a beautiful pink sari at a white elephant sale. Its teal and gold border became the border on this wall quilt that uses two sizes of fabric foundation-pieced Flying Geese blocks. The square blocks and the borders were reinforced with fusible interfacing.

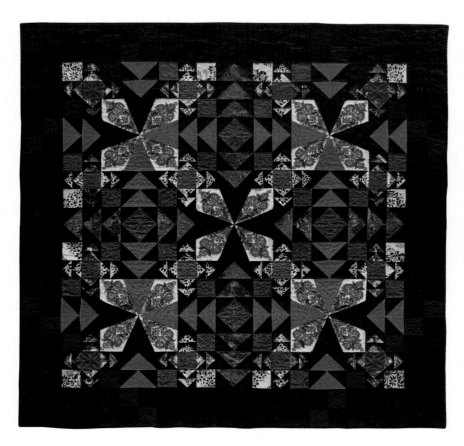

KAMEEZ, 42″ × 42″,
pieced by Julia McLeod,
machine quilted by Sue Fox

Kameez is so named because its beautifully embroidered focus fabric was cut from an Indian tunic, known as a *kameez*. The kameez is typically paired with salwar pants. Other silks from boxer shorts, neckties, and a silk evening skirt play supporting roles.

CURIOUS CURVES, 20˝ × 20˝, by Designed, pieced, and quilted by Julia McLeod

Curious Curves uses bias strips of necktie silks and the freestyle fabric foundation piecing technique described in Freestyle Fabric Foundation Piecing (page 57).

I LOVE THE SILK, 23½″ × 23½″,
by Barbara Mende Jolley,
Round Lake, Illinois; 2022

Barbara's use of stunning silks in gold
tones makes this quilt glow. The fine
black and white striped border ties
in beautifully with prints used in the
blocks.

SILKY FLYING GEESE, 20″ × 20″,
by Kathy Addington,
Marina, California; 2023

Kathy's beautiful rendition of 'Geese
Crossing' uses an array of upcycled silk
fabrics.

Wall Art Quilt, 14˝ × 14˝,
by Lori Wisheropp,
Sacramento California; 2022

Lori's directional flying geese are made with gradated colors of silk sari fabric, highlighting a treasured family brooch in the center.

STARTING WITH SILK,
20¼˝ × 20¼˝, by Helen Egerton,
Monterey California; 2023

Helen's class project from my workshop 'Starting with Silk' used 10 neckties and one scrap silk piece.

GOLDEN CROSSING, 17¼″ × 17¼″,
by Kristen Lauster,
Schenectady, New York; 2022

Notice how the placement of Kristen's golden geese creates one large square in the center of the piece. Her addition of beads in the center and along the binding adds another level of shine.

SILKY BLUES AND PURPLES,
16½″ × 16½″, by Polly Matsuoka,
Santa Barbara, California; 2023

Polly made this piece following my 'Starting with Silk' workshop. The butterfly print was from a thrifted silk blouse.

Pillow Cover, 18″ × 18″, by Kathrin Brown,
Carmel Valley, California; 2023

A deep wine red acts as a framework for Kathrin's scrappy
palette of grays, purples and pinks.

BLUE SKIES, Blue Ties, 17″ × 17″, by Nancy Sumner,
Tiburon, California; 2023

The appearance of a little red paisley adds interest to
Nancy's blue and cream pillow. The addition of piping is a
lovely detail.

Silk Pillow Cover, 18″ × 18″ by Celeste Willat,
Tiburon, California; 2023

Celeste's choice of fabric for the flying geese looks like
iridescent abalone shell.

DEBBIE'S GEESE, 18″ × 18″, by Debbie Basile,
Rocklin CA; 2023

I love Debbie's use of rich purple and bright turquoise
that make the geese stand out from the crazy pieced
background.

GEESE AROUND THE BLOCK, 24″ × 24″,
by Pat Masterson,
Ventura, California; 2023

Pat created a square arrangement of the
same four strips of geese used in Geese
Crossing. She then added an outer border of
crazy pieced necktie silks.

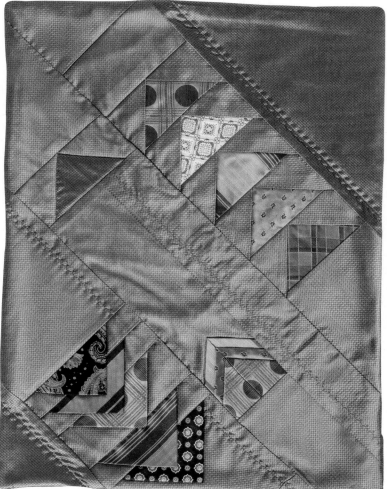

GOING FOR COFFEE, 18″ × 24″,
by Christi Sutphen,
Pacific Grove, California; 2023

Christi took her flight of silk geese and placed
them in a modern, masculine composition,
mounting the piece on a canvas frame.

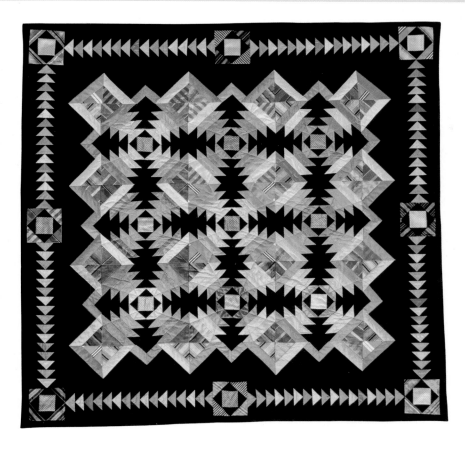

HOME IS NOT A PLACE, 48″ × 48″,
by Mary Spadaro,
Cambridge Massachusetts; 2021

Mary made her first orange and
black blocks in my class 'Piecing the
Pineapple'. The addition of splashes
of turquoise, lilac and gold, and the
cleverly engineered border make this
quilt a real beauty.

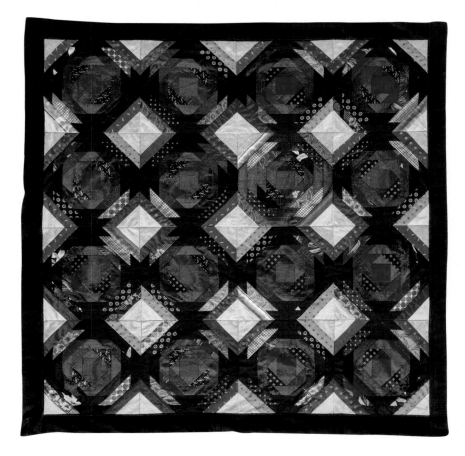

MOOD INDIGO, 43″ × 43″,
by Anna Erickson,
Oakland California; 2023

Anna's coloring of her pineapple block
surprised me when she made it in my
pineapple workshop. We used the
iphone app 'PhotoCollage' to create
a mock up of what a quilt would look
like using 16 of those curious blocks.
Anna went for it, completing this
gorgeous silk throw.

HANDSOME PINEAPPLES, 36″ × 36″, by Kathryn King Rector, Horseshoe Bay, Texas; machine quilted by Leslie Sparks, Burnet, Texas; 2023

The name says it all: Traditional necktie silks are supported by two shades of deep red dupioni silk in this good-looking quilt. Kathryn's use of sashing adds a graphic grid to the composition.

GRANDMOTHER'S FAN, 23″ x 23″,
by Karren Lusignan,
Auburn, California; 2022

Purples and blues dominate the color
scheme of Karren's version of 'Flying
Circus'. The smart choice to include a
flash of gold really adds visual interest.

FABMO FANCY, 28½″ x 28½″,
by Randa Mulford,
Mountain View, California; 2021

Randa's quilt is a variation of my
'Flying Circus' pattern, featuring
embroidered medallions added to the
corners, center and borders. Fabmo
is a wonderful resource in Sunnyvale,
California, for designer samples,
fabrics and notions.
Visit www.fabmo.org

SILK FANS, 25˝ × 25˝, by Peggie Wormington, Colfax, California; 2022

Peggie made these rich, blue fan blocks in a virtual workshop with me. She chose to set them on point and added a scrappy border of 1˝ × 2˝ Flying Geese.

Postscript

I hope this book has inspired you to bring a little *Patchwork Luxe* into your life and make a silk quilt! I encourage you to *use* those precious textiles you've been storing carefully for years. Now, you have a handful of techniques that will allow you to build stable, accurate blocks with confidence.

I wish you many hours of enjoyable sewing!

Templates

Photocopy the required template(s) to begin your project.

If the patterns need to be enlarged, the enlargement percentage is provided with the pattern. Use that percentage on your home or copyshop copier. If the pattern is getting larger than one sheet of paper, copy the pattern in overlapping quadrants and tile them together.

To access all of the full-size patterns for this book, type the web address below into your browser window.

tinyurl.com/11585-patterns-download

Using Downloaded Templates

Print directly from the browser window or download the template.

Review the complete instructions for printing and tiling included in the pattern download PDF.

- To print at home, print the letter-size pages, selecting 100% size on the printer. Use dashed/dotted lines to trim, layer, and tape together pages as needed.

- To print at a copyshop, save the full-size pages to a thumb drive or email them to your local copyshop for printing.

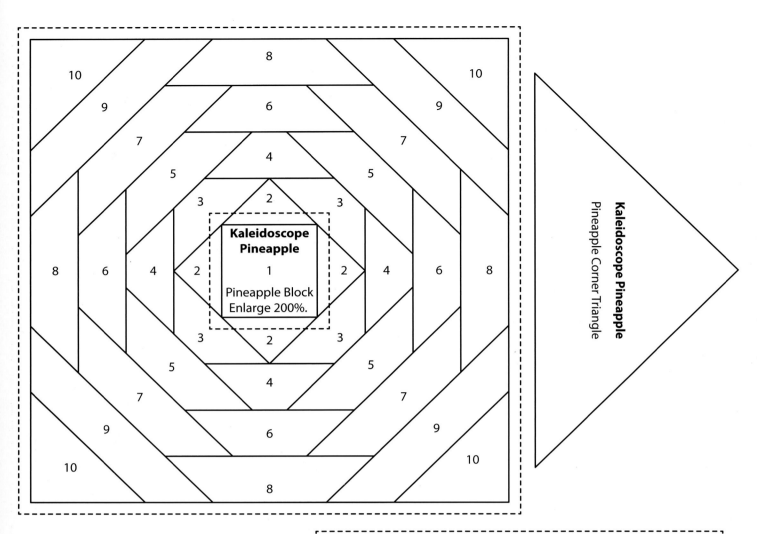

Kaleidoscope Pineapple

Pineapple Block
Enlarge 200%.

8 10 9 7 6 4 5 3 2 3 5 7 9 10 8 6 4 2 2 4 6 8 1 2 2 4 6 8 3 2 3 5 4 5 7 6 7 9 9 10 8 10

Kaleidoscope Pineapple
Pineapple Corner Triangle

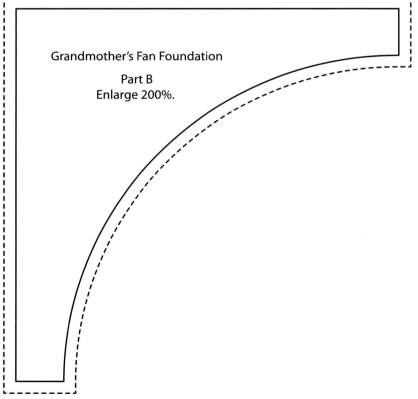

Grandmother's Fan Foundation

Part B
Enlarge 200%.

Full size templates are available for download. See Templates (page 119) for download and enlargement instructions.

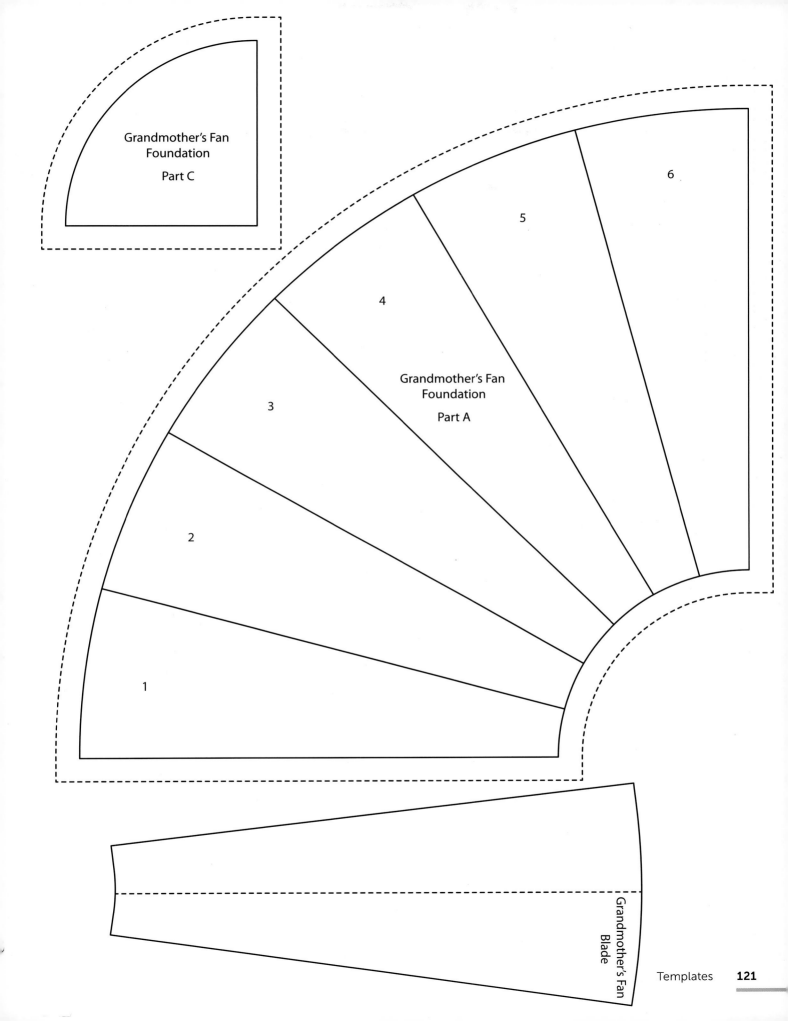

Grandmother's Fan
Foundation

Part C

6

5

4

Grandmother's Fan
Foundation

Part A

3

2

1

Grandmother's Fan
Blade

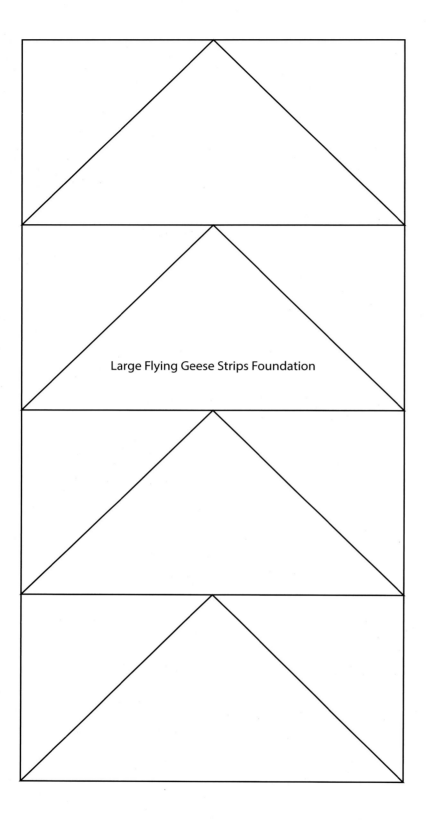

Large Flying Geese Strips Foundation

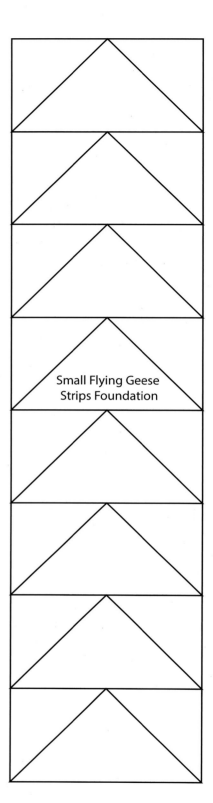

Small Flying Geese Strips Foundation

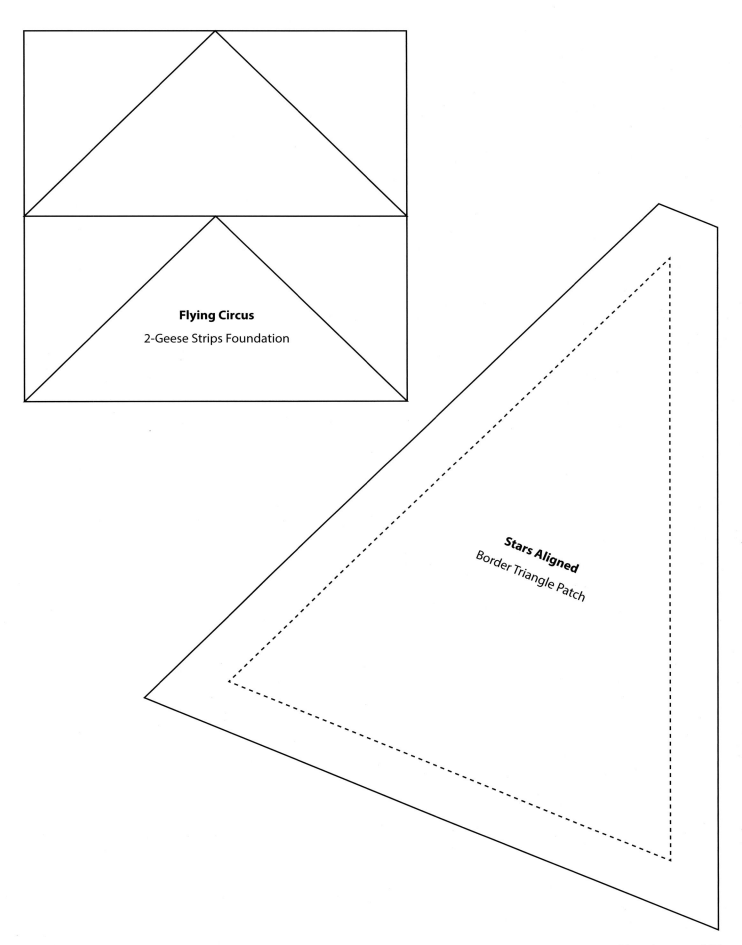

Flying Circus

2-Geese Strips Foundation

Stars Aligned
Border Triangle Patch

Full size templates are available for download. See Templates (page 119) for download and enlargement instructions.

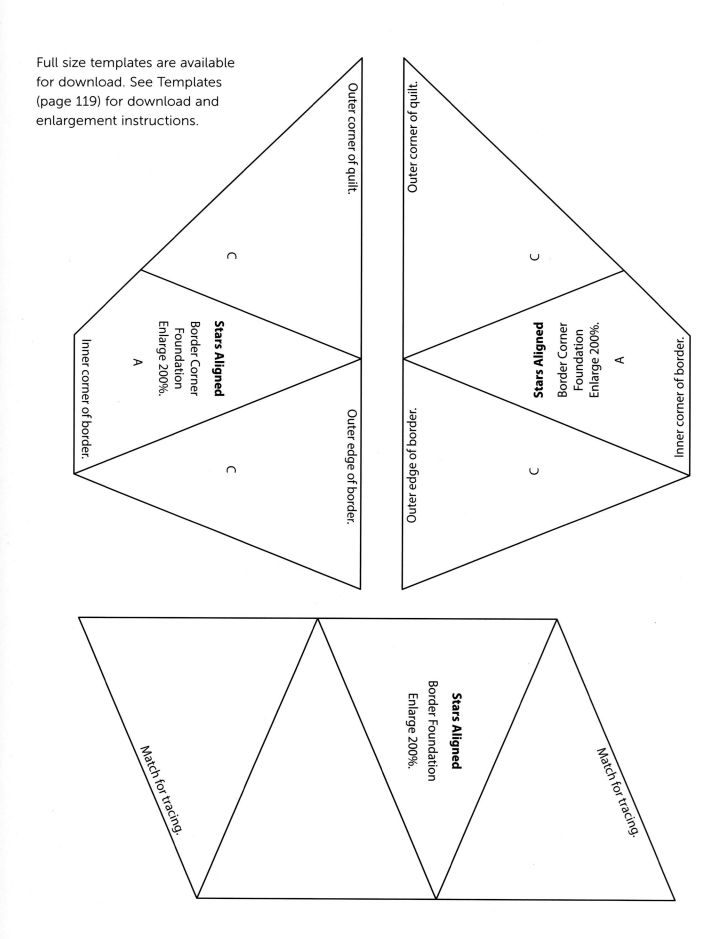

Outer corner of quilt.

Outer corner of quilt.

C

C

Stars Aligned
Border Corner
Foundation
Enlarge 200%.

Stars Aligned
Border Corner
Foundation
Enlarge 200%.

A

A

Inner corner of border.

Inner corner of border.

Outer edge of border.

Outer edge of border.

C

C

Match for tracing.

Match for tracing.

Stars Aligned
Border Foundation
Enlarge 200%.

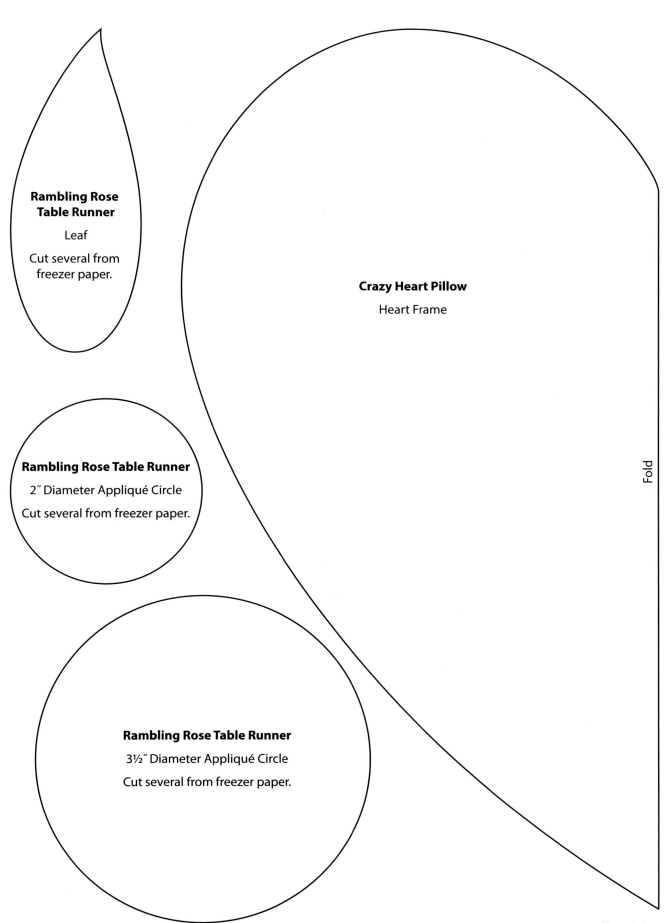

Rambling Rose Table Runner

Leaf

Cut several from freezer paper.

Crazy Heart Pillow

Heart Frame

Fold

Rambling Rose Table Runner

2″ Diameter Appliqué Circle

Cut several from freezer paper.

Rambling Rose Table Runner

3½″ Diameter Appliqué Circle

Cut several from freezer paper.

Kaleidoscope Pineapple Coloring Page

About the Author

Born and raised in England, Julia McLeod earned a degree in textile design and worked in the British textile industry in Yorkshire and Scotland. From a design job on London's Savile Row—the heart of the men's tailoring industry—she relocated to New York City for a menswear career there. America has been her home ever since.

After quilting with cotton for many years, Julia developed a passion for sewing with upcycled silks from neckties, kimonos, and saris. She has mastered techniques that tame silk's tendencies to fray, slip, and stretch. Julia teaches and lectures nationally, internationally, and as a course instructor on the innovative and interactive platform Creative Spark Online Learning (by C&T Publishing). Her quilts have won awards in the UK and in the United States. Julia lives in the San Francisco Bay area of California.

Visit Julia online and follow on social media!

Website: juliamcleodquilts.com

Instagram: @juliamcleodquilts

Facebook: /JuliaMcLeodQuilts

YouTube: /@juliamcleodquilts

Creative Spark: creativespark.ctpub.com

CREATIVE SPARK
ONLINE LEARNING

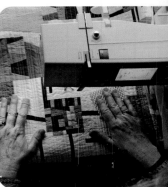

Quilting courses to become an expert quilter...

From their studio to yours, Creative Spark instructors are teaching you how to create and become a master of your craft. So not only do you get a look inside their creative space, you also get to be a part of engaging courses that would typically be a one or multi-day workshop from the comfort of your home.

Creative Spark is not your one-size-fits-all online learning experience. We welcome you to be who you are, share, create, and belong.

Scan for a gift from us!

creativespark.ctpub.com